Lessons
To Nourish the Soul:
John

By
Rev. Marjorie E. Palmer

Table of Contents

John 1: 14 NIV

14 *The Word became flesh and made his dwelling among us. We have seen his glory, the glory of the one and only Son, who came from the Father, full of grace and truth.*

John 1: 14b
'And we beheld his glory'

POINTS OF LIGHT

God came into the world, took on flesh, and lived among us to show us the way Home. That is the Incarnation, what we celebrate at Christmas. Coming to earth and becoming one with us is what God did.

Scripture tells us about Mary and Joseph going to Bethlehem to welcome the Holy Child.

We spend much time and thinking and decorating and celebrating for that part of Christmas. But that isn't all there is.

The other side of Christmas, which comes on January 6th, is Epiphany.

That event is much less understood, mentioned, or celebrated.

Oh, I'm sure we can speak about the Three Kings, or the Three Wisemen—the Magi—who traveled far in search of the newborn King of the Jews. We can probably say the names of the Wisemen: Caspar, Melchior, and Balthazar. We have memories of seeing them many times bringing up the end of a Christmas pageant. The three trudge slowly up the aisle, their very presence speaking loudly of their position in life as men of education, means, and power. They came carrying wonderful gifts to the Christ Child.

The picture of the Three is the picture we need to consider today.

The Magi began their journey because of two things: They came because they read the prophecy in the Hebrew Bible about the One who was to come, and they saw the star.

At one time I didn't really believe that they could have known those prophetic scriptures, because who else could have read the Hebrew sacred texts except the Hebrews? But then I learned about the Septuagint (LXX), which is the Hebrew Bible translated into Greek. The Septuagint was translated some 300 years before Christ's birth, so those sacred texts were available to many people beyond the Israelites. (Somebody, somewhere, realized that those sacred writing of the Hebrews might be valuable for others to read, and so the effort of translating the material was made.)

The Magi read of the coming of the child, and the saw the star in the sky. When they found the star in the sky, they realized they could follow it and find the king. And they began their trek to the place where the child could be found.

The picture of the Magi coming to present themselves before the newborn child is a touching and wonderful picture. Here we see these three great men bowing before the tiny child, the Incarnate One. They humbled themselves before him and gave him gifts befitting their station.

The picture of the Magi at the manger is what we call 'an Epiphany'. An Epiphany is a moment when some important things come together for us. Miss Sylvia called it an 'Aha moment' the other day. She's right, but it's not just any 'aha moment'. It's a special 'aha moment'.

An Epiphany is a moment of clarity;
- a moment when we experience being in God's presence;
- a realization that we've been touched by God.

I believe that every Christian has had a moment of Epiphany! If we are followers of Christ, then we've had to have a moment, and hopefully more than one, when we have felt

- we've been in the presence of Christ,
- that contact has been make,

- that something REAL and IMPORTANT has taken place,
- and it makes a difference; it changes our lives.

We know the epiphany moments of many Christians.

I suppose being in Jesus' presence Jesus followers had moments of epiphany every day. They saw Jesus do miracles that clearly spoke of his connection to God. Jesus used to say, *'if you don't believe me for my words, at least look at the things I'm doing (that you can see) and believe because of them'.*

Think of the time when Jesus stood up in the boat and commanded the terrible storm to be calm … and all was suddenly quiet. The disciples had a moment of epiphany. They asked one another, *'What sort of man is this, that even the winds and the sea obey him?'* (Mk 8:27)

We could talk all day about those times when Jesus brought moments of epiphany to those who followed him during his ministry— feeding 5000 people; bringing sight to the man born blind; healing ten lepers at once; raising people from the dead … and on and on. Those were each moments of epiphany.

But what about folks who came later? What about people who never had the opportunity to personally see or hear Jesus? How might they experience an epiphany?

Take Saul. We remember Saul. He was a very angry man, a man possessed with one purpose: to stamp out all the Followers of the Way. He did his darndest to imprison and make life scary and dangerous for the young church. Then, as he was travelling to Damascus to bring more terror on the followers there, Saul was thrown to the ground and suddenly blinded. And he met Jesus right then and there on the road. Jesus spoke to him and proved to Saul that he was alive! Saul's epiphany led him to become the greatest missionary ever and the writer of half the books in New Testament.

John Wesley also had a notable moment of Epiphany. Listen to Wesley's own words about it:

"In the evening I went very unwillingly to a society in Aldersgate Street, where one was reading Luther's preface to the Epistle to the Romans. About a quarter before nine, while the leader was describing the change which God works in the heart through faith in Christ, I felt my heart strangely warmed. I felt I did trust in Christ alone for salvation; and an assurance

*was given me that He had taken away my sins,
even mine, and saved me from the law of sin
and death."*

Wesley's epiphany moment happened
shortly before he began preaching out of
doors, traveling across all of England, Wales,
Scotland, and Ireland. The Wesleyan
movement touched many thousands of lives.
He sent lay preachers to the colonies to preach
the good news here. Wesley's movement
made such a difference in so many lives that
historians tell us that England didn't suffer a
political revolution like the French did, because
so many people had come to faith in Christ
through the Methodists!

St. John tells us that when the Word was
made flesh and lived among them, that is when
Jesus, the God/Man, was present with the
people, 'We beheld his glory.' Jesus' followers
'beheld his glory.'

They beheld ... they saw ... they
recognized something in Jesus that was very,
very special. They saw in him a man who was
perfect. He had no flaws. The more they saw
him and heard him and watched him the more
they realized there was something about him
that was new and wonderful.

Remember the guards on duty when Jesus died. They experienced the earthquake and the heaven darkening and roaring. They exclaimed, *'Surely this man was the son of God!'* (Mt 27:54)

'We beheld his glory.' They beheld his glory.

Glory is a word that is a bit hard to define. I suppose we picture 'glory' related to a halo or bright lights behind someone. But glory is about seeing Who God is or Who Christ is.

Glory is recognizing God's power and authority and grandeur and might. It is a moment of awe when we are struck with an overwhelming feeling of greatness.

I think the best picture of Christ's glory was at the resurrection. That was the quintessential moment of epiphany. At that moment Jesus' followers saw something they'd begun to see before. They'd begun to see his glory, his connection to God, in all the things that occurred during Jesus' ministry, but when he rose and showed himself to then alive, they had their great epiphany.

Remember how they changed? How they changed from deeply depressed and seriously in pain people? They changed because of the epiphany, the realization of who Jesus is … completely connected to God!

It changed their lives forever.

That's what an epiphany does. With the Incarnation, sending Jesus to earth to live among us, God did a wonderful thing. The gift he gave us is ours to open and enjoy.

Epiphany is what we do about the incarnation.

Epiphany may be an aha moment, but it is not one that is a total surprise. The Magi had already set out to find the infant king. They had their gifts with them for the child. They were actively seeking the child. When they finally came to the place where the child lay, they experienced their epiphany. It was even greater than they had imagined. Somehow, they saw in that little child the hope for the nations. They knew in their hearts that the child was sent from God. They knelt before him and gave him their gifts.

An epiphany is about seeking Christ, spending the time and energy to find him. It's about humbling ourselves before him, and giving him our hearts.

That's our response to the wonderful gift that had been sent to us.

The gift of Christ is waiting for us to claim Him.

Like the Magi, we can search for the child, for our LORD. We can most easily find him by following the 'points of light' that are in many places.

What are these 'points of light?

The Magi followed the great star in the sky to find the Christ Child. It was a physical phenomenon, easy to behold. It compelled them to follow it.

The 'points of light' that lead us to know Christ are the 'means of grace' we've heard about before. The 'points of light include:

- searching the scriptures;
- prayer;
- Holy Communion;
- fasting;
- Christian conferencing;
- healthy living;
- doing good;
- visiting the sick and imprisoned;
- feeding and clothing the needy,
- using money wisely;
- working for justice.

There are lots of ways to help us experience an epiphany. Did you notice that in that group of items all of them involve our doing something? It is not a passive thing to have an epiphany. It's not life being hit by lightning. It is something we do to put ourselves in the way of God's Grace. God sent the son to the world to connect with us, but we have to do our parts. We must put ourselves in the way of God's action in this world if we want to experience an epiphany in our lives.

Then! When we have had such moments, we, ourselves, can be a point of light for others.

<u>WHY CHRISTMAS!</u>

Today is the First Sunday of Christmas, but the world has stopped singing Christmas carols. The stores have now put out the New Year's Eve colors and items, and all the trappings of Christmas are soon to be gone. The red and greed that was ubiquitous before has been changed out for blue, and silver, and white   . The carols have been given over to 'elevator music.'

I really wonder why we Christians are still 'doing Christmas'. Why are we still participating in the holiday that has clearly been taken over the pagan world?

There's one story that's actually pretty new to the Christmas milieu. I'm talking about a Santa story with a twist.

I can remember when I was in fourth grace, my teacher, Miss Whiteford, came into class with a <u>Family Circle</u> magazine and read the story <u>How the Grinch Stole Christmas.</u> Our whole class loved the story of the old geezer who had nothing to say but 'Bah Humbug!' about Christmas, and how he tried with all his might to stop Christmas from coming. But somehow, even after he had literally stolen all the stuff of Christmas from every household in Who-Ville— the trees, the presents, the food, the décor— Christmas still came!

Remember the Grinch had just returned to his home at the top of Mt. Crumpit, and he knew the people would be awaking to discover their loss, and he expected them to cry loudly because of it.

[hold up the book and read from Grinch books]

"Then the Whos down in Who-Ville will all cry BOO-HOO!"
'That's a noise', grinned the Grinch,
'That I simply MUST hear!'
So he paused, And the Grinch put his hand to his ear.
And he did hear a sound rising over the snow.
It started in low, then it started to grow…
But the sound wasn't sad!
Why, the sound sounded merry!
It couldn't be so!
But was merry! VERY!
He stared down at Who-ville!
Then he shook!
What he saw was a shocking surprise!
Every Who down in Who-ville, the tall and the small,
Was singing! Without any presents at all!
He HADN'T stopped Christmas from coming!
IT CAME!
Somehow or other, it came just the same!"
Even without any of the stuff of Christmas, Christmas came just the same.

What is it about Christmas that makes Christmas 'Christmas?'

If we went around this room today and interviewed each person here and asked them, 'What makes Christmas 'Christmas' for you?' we'd get different answers. We'd get comments like

- Being with family
- The excitement of all the presents being opened up on Christmas morning.
- Some favorite family traditions
- Maybe some special meal or a favorite dish
- Maybe it's taking out the decorations, cherishing those favorite, old pieces
- Maybe it's the music
- Or the cards we get from far distant friends
- Maybe it's all those things put together.

There are many things we might think of that really make Christmas 'Christmas' for us, but isn't there more? Isn't there a deeper meaning of Christmas? Isn't there something more important than nostalgia and good food?

Let's look at it a little differently. Let's start with which came first-Christmas or Easter? That's a trick question. In the calendar year, of course, Easter comes first. We celebrate Easter in the springtime, and Christmas is nearly the last week of the year. Easter was celebrated first from the beginning of the church.

The followers of Jesus celebrated His rising from the dead every first day of the week from

Pentecost on. So we could easily say that Easter came first. It came nearly 400 years before the first Christmas was celebrated.

Back then the pagan world had their own celebrations, and the worst of them all was the Feast of Bacchus, the feast of the god of wine. This feast came during the mid-winter, the darkest time of the year. The feast was a long, drunken orgy, and the Christians, of course, couldn't participate in it. So they decided to celebrate the birth of Jesus, who is the Light of the world, in the darkest time of the year.

And so the celebration of Christmas was begun.

It wasn't' just another holiday or time to party, the Christians had a very great event in mind. They were celebrating what St. John called the incarnation.

John wrote, '…*and the Word was made flesh and dwelt among us.' (John 1:12)*

The Word is Christ.

John wrote, *'In the beginning the Word was God.'* (John 1:1)

That's quite some statement! 'The Word was God. The Greek word for Word is LOGOS, which means 'language…infused with truth, order, and wisdom.'

'In the beginning was the Word and the Word was God and the Word was with God. He was

with God in the beginning.   All things came into being through him, and without him not one thing came into being. What has come into being ⁴in him was life, and the life was the light of all people'. (John 1:1-3)

It is that Word that was made flesh and dwelt among us.

We hear the word 'incarnation' but we don't throw it around much. It's not part of our everyday conversation. Incarnation literally means something that has taken on flesh.

The wooden puppet Pinocchio had a dream of becoming incarnate. He didn't use that word, but that's what he wanted to be. More than anything he wanted to become real—a real flesh and blood boy with real feelings. That picture might help us to get the picture of 'incarnation.'

The Word was made flesh.

That is such a simple sentence, yet it is one of the greatest truths in history, perhaps the greatest of all.

The deal is that God came into this world as a human person and lived a life as a human just like each one of us.

Now there are some folks who don't actually believe in the Virgin birth of Christ. That is to say they accept Jesus as the Son of God, because they see God affirming Jesus' ministry through the resurrection, but they can't make the leap of faith about the Virgin birth.

- That Jesus' Father is Almighty God

- That Mary, Jesus' mother, conceived the child via the Holy Spirit.

- And the child was therefore completely God and completely human from the very first moment.

Those who only see Jesus as the adoptive Son of God are missing the really BIG thing about the incarnation. If John is right and the Word was made flesh that says tremendous things about WHO JESUS IS! He was

- With God when the earth and heaven were formed

- In him God and creation have been fused...put together.

- In Jesus of Nazareth we find the completion of all things.

Before the INCARNATION there were the two: God and creation. God is completely other than creation. (There are some people who think that God is IN everything ... that the entire universe is what God is, but that is not Christian thinking.

- God is NOT the universe
- God is the maker of the universe

- God is the mind behind all the wonder of the universe
- But God is NOT the universe

Then comes the Christ, the Incarnate One. In him all that was made is brought together with God. In Him all creation is gathered together with God. Does that not mean that in Christ we have the KINGDOM!

- Isn't He the Beginning and the End?
- Isn't He the Alpha and the Omega?
- Isn't He the final answer to all our problems?
- Isn't He the One in whom all our hopes can rest?
- Isn't Jesus our friend, our counselor, our redeemer, our King … and so much more!

In Jesus Christ we have the two together, and that means that whatever happened to Jesus connected to and occurred to all creation. Think about it. Jesus is the true connection between heaven and earth! In Him there is a new thing that brings everything together. In Him all the Universe has a new meaning. In Him Hope is perfected!

So have we got a reason to celebrate Jesus' birth? You bet!

Christmas started out to be a 'counter-culture' event, something that would stand in opposition to the worldly practice of drunken orgies that were taking place back then. The Christians would be different. They would celebrate the coming of the Light of Christ into this dark world.

But over the many years the world has picked up on Christmas and take it over. Christmas now belongs to the world. Christmas, as far as the world knows, is all about Santa and magical elves and flying reindeer, and if you don't believe in those things Christmas will vanish forever!

Bah Humbug! We know that's not what Christmas is about.

The story of the Grinch tells a real truth. It points out that Christmas is not dependent on boxes, bells, and bows. Christmas resides firmly in the hearts of believers.

Can you imagine for a minute us finding ourselves in a very difficult position at Christmastime? Do you suppose that we'd just simply cancel Christmas and continue on as if there was not a reason to celebrate? Could we really skip Christmas and not notice it?

Even if we can't afford to buy a 20 pound bird or send out 100 Christmas cards or somehow we'd lost all our holiday décor, do you supposed we'd just forget about Christmas?

I don't think so! We can sing the carols and join our hand and hearts together in thanking god for the miracle of sending us His Son.

Remember the picture of the Who-Villians as they gathered together hand in hand singing together. They are a beautiful picture of Christian life. Dr. Seuss doesn't try to explain why Christmas came to the people, but he does describe HOW Christians act when they are challenged. They know that there is more than bows and boxes, and food that make up our faith. The trimmings may be fun and exciting, but they are only secondary to the real reason for Christmas, and that is joining together to sing praise to the LORD.

29 The next day he *saw Jesus coming to him and *said, "Behold, the Lamb of God who takes away the sin of the world! 30 This is He on behalf of whom I said, 'After me comes a Man who [a]has a higher rank than I, for He existed before me.' 31 I did not recognize [b]Him, but so that He might be manifested to Israel, I came baptizing [c]in water." 32 John testified saying, "I have seen the Spirit descending as a dove out of heaven, and He remained upon Him. 33 I did not recognize [d]Him, but He who sent me to baptize [e]in water said to me, 'He upon whom you see the Spirit descending and remaining upon Him, this is the One who baptizes [f]in the Holy Spirit.' 34 I myself have seen, and have testified that this is the Son of God."

35 Again the next day John was standing [g]with two of his disciples, 36 and he looked at Jesus as He walked, and *said, "Behold, the Lamb of God!" 37 The two disciples heard him speak, and they followed Jesus. 38 And Jesus turned and saw them following, and *said to them, "What

do you seek?" They said to Him, "Rabbi (which translated means Teacher), where are You staying?" 39 He *said to them, "Come, and you will see." So they came and saw where He was staying; and they stayed with Him that day, for it was about the [h]tenth hour. 40 One of the two who heard John speak and followed Him, was Andrew, Simon Peter's brother. 41 He *found first his own brother Simon and *said to him, "We have found the Messiah" (which translated means [i]Christ). 42 He brought him to Jesus. Jesus looked at him and said, "You are Simon the son of [j]John; you shall be called Cephas" (which is translated [k]Peter).

"**COME AND SEE**"

Sometimes, when you are looking for something it can become challenge to find it, to find just the thing that you want. You find that just looking has become a real search. And sometimes the search is as much fun as the actual item searched for.

There's a saying, actually a silly saying, that when you have a tour in Germany, you either go home with a new baby or a cuckoo clock. Since Dave and I have had four babies born overseas, which is all the babies that we have had, the last time we moved to Germany, we thought maybe we ought to get us a clock.

There are a number of manufacturers of cuckoo clocks and many choices of clocks to choose from. Some clocks just tell time and cuckoo on the hour. Some play music, too. You might guess that I would want one that has music on it.

As we began looking for the right clock, we discovered that 98% of the clocks with music played two pieces and one of the two is Edelweiss. (You know-----*singing a bit of Edelweiss*....) That's very cute and appropriate for something that comes from Germany, but I thought that since I would be hearing this same music 12 times a day for the rest of my life, it might be nice to hear something different. Edelweiss is a rather trite tune.

And so the search began. Whenever we were out on some sort of trip, we'd check the various clock shops and tourist shops, looking for a nice clock that did not have the tune Edelweiss in it. We even traveled to DAS HAUS DEM THOUSAND UHREN, the House of a Thousand Clocks, and several other big clock shops in the village where they are all made. No luck. The clocks we liked, which had dancers and much gingerbread on the front had Edelweiss inside! We asked if the manufacturers would change the music box for a different one, which we would chose, but the answer was, *"Leider nicht"*. "Sorry, no."

After months of looking, we did find the right clock. It is everything that we wanted, with a goodly price to accompany it. It hangs in our kitchen and plays very nicely. I really think the process of looking for the clock was part of the fun of finally finding it.

DO WE KNOW WHAT WE ARE LOOKING FOR?

We spend our lives looking--- for various things. Sometimes we spend great time, effort and resources searching, searching, hoping to find the something that will fill us ... the thing that will answer our questions, fill the void in our lives, give us a feeling of worth or belonging, give us ... what?

Some of us look for answers in our jobs:

In our 21st century world, it is quite possible for a person to have a number of jobs during one lifetime. We do different jobs over the years. These days there is time spent in education, time for apprenticeship or OJT, time maybe for several vocations, or job changes. Nothing is static. I've heard that a person coming up today needs to figure on re-educating his/herself three or four times in the course of life. I wonder if women have an even greater challenge in finding positions, as there is often a need to be at home with little ones for a number of years, and then the process of getting into or back into the work force.

But the vocation we choose or the vocations we find ourselves occupied in, don't have the final answer for life. Some people make the mistake of making their vocations their identity. "I am the boss of such and such." "I am a teacher or professor at some school." "I wrote books; I am an author." "I am the owner of whatever business." "I am the expert in whatever field," and so on.

Jobs are good and useful; they provide income and challenge; they help us grow. But they don't fill the need we have for finding meaning and belonging that is within each of us.

Maybe we look for the answer in our friends:

Friends are so wonderful. Thank goodness for friends. Friends are good for company, good for sharing. Friends add depth and richness to our lives. Friends are good for enjoying time together. Where would we be without friends? But friends, in themselves, are not the answer. Friends can't fill every void in our lives. Friends can't be everything to us. We need more.

Many of us look for answers in our children or families:

They are great gifts. They give us such richness. Just ask any parent around here to tell us about his/her family, and we shall be filled with pictures and stories about the beautiful family we've been given.

We grow in so many ways because of our children. We learn from our children; we learn to think of others before ourselves; we learn to see beyond ourselves when we have children to be responsible for. We try to pass on the values we cherish to our children. We see their gifts and work to help them develop their gifts. We can count our children, and our grandchildren, as jewels in our crown.

Surely we are thankful for our children. Yet they cannot be the answer, either. Our children are ours for only a portion of our lives. I think God has only lent our children to us for a season, so that we can nurture them. But children must strike out on their own, eventually.

We can be filled with the joy of our children, but they do not hold the answer to what we seek.

For many of us the closest person we will ever know is our spouse. What a gift … and a challenge. Spouses, (or should it be spice?)-- having one, being one--is definitely part of God's plan. Our spouses are given to us as helpmates, as growth-mates, for surely we grow most through our spouses. "Spice" provide so many gifts to us—companionship, children, income, home--yet they are not the answer, either. Some of us have looked to our spice to fill all out needs. But they can't. Our spouses are wonderful gifts from God, but they are not the answer, either.

If we rely on any of these good things—job, family, friends, home, stuff, even spouses—to find the answers to life, we will find disappointment. We will find that there is still something more that we really need.

There's another list of things some of us have used to find the answers. Those things include bigger cars, newer, bigger homes, fancier clothes, or even the stuff that's supposed to dull the pain and anxiety of living—drink, drugs, all of that. We know those things won't bring answers, yet we certainly hear and read about people abusing them every day.

"WHAT ARE YOU LOOKING FOR?"

That's the question Jesus asked two of John's disciples, as they followed Jesus one day.

John's disciples had started out as ordinary men—ordinary fishermen. They followed in the steps of their fathers and brothers by fishing. They learned to rise early, to handle a boat, and mend their nets. They learned how to be patient as they waited for the catch. They learned how to haul in the lines and handle the fish. They learned how to market the fish. They even learned how to get their fish to the larger market in Jerusalem, where the city people would pay more.

The disciples were fishermen. They were also young men, who had their lives in front of them.

They had met John; perhaps they had heard of him and the work he was doing by the Jordan. They left their nets and went after John and became John's disciples. They were with John and saw and heard him daily. They knew his message well—that everyone needed to repent. They had heard John's message every day while they were with him. And they knew his witness--that there would be One coming after him, who would take away the sins of the world.

As disciples of John, they had left their worldly things. They learned about the Messiah, the One who would come and change the world.

Then one day, John pointed to a man passing by and called him the "Lamb of God." The disciples knew when John gave that man the title, that he was a very special person.

The Jews knew about lambs, and what a Passover Lamb was about. Every spring every Jewish family would buy a sheep or a lamb and they would tie it up in their yard and prepare it for the very special Passover meal. The lamb was washed up clean and fed and petted and cared for over the several days before the big day. Then on the afternoon of the Passover, the father of the family would slit the throat of the animal and then divide the meat among the families, the needy folks, keeping a good piece for his own family to cook and eat.

The Jews did this every year in memory of the great Passover long before when God told Moses to prepare the Israelites for their escape from slavery. Back then God told the Israelites to paint their doorposts with the blood of lambs and thereby avoid the angel of death who would pass over their homes. When the death angel saw the blood of the lamb on their doors, it would Passover that household. But it took the life of the first born of every Egyptian household. That was a sacred story, the one, which preceded their release from bondage in Egypt and put their people on the path back to the Promised Land. The Lamb of God was the name of the One who would be that innocent creature that once before had provided life for their people. The Lamb of God would somehow provide salvation for Israel. He was someone that they wanted to know more about.

Two of John's disciples set off to follow this Jesus. They didn't approach him immediately.

Their initial plan seemed to be to follow at a respectful distance to see where he might be going.

I have to wonder if John, himself, would not have been tempted to leave his own ministry and to follow Jesus? Could he not, possibly, have some part in Jesus' ministry? Of course, when we come up with that sort of speculation, we can't really answer it, as there is no answer in Scripture. It remains speculation. But John may have realized that he was in a sensitive position, and closer association with Jesus might have brought trouble to Jesus' ministry before it really got to take off. John did not follow Jesus. He had to be satisfied with sending his disciples to him. I believe that John felt the loss of his disciples, as they took their next step, the one that led away from him.

These two disciples of John included Andrew and quite probably John, son of Zebedee. As they followed Jesus, they seemed to hang back, perhaps thinking they could learn more about him, whom John had been pointed out to them.

Then Jesus turned, looked at the two who were following him and asked them, "What are you looking for?"

Jesus knew better than the disciples did what they were looking for. They simply answered Jesus' question, "Rabbi, where are you staying?"

By calling Jesus "Rabbi," the disciples indicated that they understood that Jesus was a teacher, and that they were open to learning from him, perhaps becoming his disciples.

Then Jesus answered, saying, Come and see.

Come and see....

Come, get to know me

Get to know me and the One who sent me.

Come, become my friend

I will be the best friend you will ever have.

In me you can place your trust.

In me you can lay down your burdens.

Come, hear what I have to say

Come hear about the Kingdom of God

Come hear my command to love one another

Come hear my call to discipleship

Come, witness my ministry

Come witness these next few years

Come witness the miracles I will do

Come witness the healings I will bring

Come, learn

-

Come learn my ways and my thoughts

Come learn about my Father in Heaven

Come learn ....

Come unto me, all ye who labor and are heavy laden, and I will give you rest.

"Let anyone who is thirsty come to me, [38]and let the one who believes in me drink

Come and see

What I am about to do.

See me heal the sick

Feed the hungry

Bring good news to the poor

Proclaim release to the captives

And freedom to the oppressed

Hear me proclaim the year of the Lord's favor to all.

Come and see how I will turn the world upside down

Come and see how I will fill you with my Spirit

Come and see

Come, see, discover for yourselves

discover who I am;

discover that I am the Lamb of God

discover what I can do for you

discover that in me, you will find eternal life

discover who you are in me.

Discover how you are more fully you when you are in me.

The two disciples of John were Jesus' first followers. Andrew quickly brought his brother, Simon to Jesus and he became the disciple we know as Peter. Eventually there were many followers. Jesus called some individually and invited them to follow him. Others came on their own.

The size of Jesus' following seems to have fluctuated. John reports in his Gospel that there was even a time later in Jesus' ministry when many of his followers left him. They had decided that what Jesus was asking of them was going to be difficult, and they left.

When those followers left, Jesus looked at his inner core of followers, the twelve, and asked: "Do you also wish to go away?" and Simon Peter answered him, "Lord, to whom can we go? You have the words of eternal life. We have come to believe and know that you are the Holy One of God."

The disciples came and saw. They had found the one who filled them and made them new.

They had discovered that Jesus was what they were looking for.

Is Jesus what you are looking for? Have you given him your life? Have you pledged your complete dedication to the Lord? Have you promised to serve him and him only for the rest of your life?

Have you come to see what he has for you? Have you found that what he offers is worthwhile? Have you discovered that he offers life today and life in the world eternal?

2 *On the third day a wedding took place at Cana in Galilee. Jesus' mother was there, 2 and Jesus and his disciples had also been invited to the wedding. 3 When the wine was gone, Jesus' mother said to him, "They have no more wine."*

4 "Woman,[a] why do you involve me?" Jesus replied. "My hour has not yet come."

5 His mother said to the servants, "Do whatever he tells you."

6 Nearby stood six stone water jars, the kind used by the Jews for ceremonial washing, each holding from twenty to thirty gallons.[b]

7 Jesus said to the servants, "Fill the jars with water"; so they filled them to the brim.

8 Then he told them, "Now draw some out and take it to the master of the banquet."

They did so, 9 and the master of the banquet tasted the water that had been turned into wine. He did not realize where it had come from, though the servants who had drawn the water knew. Then he called the bridegroom aside 10 and said, "Everyone brings out the choice wine first and then the cheaper wine after the guests have had too much to drink; but you have saved the best till now."

11 What Jesus did here in Cana of Galilee was the first of the signs through which he revealed his glory; and his disciples believed in him.

LOTS IN POTS

Dave and I lived for two years in Izmir, Turkey on the Bay of Izmir, which is on the West coast of the country. It is a desertous land, not unlike Arizona, where Dave and I grew up. Desert living has its challenges; one of which is lack of water.

The city of Izmir didn't have enough water for all its needs. We discovered this fact the day we arrived in country. We flew in late in the evening and were taken to the Kordon Hotel on the waterfront, as very nice hotel where American soldiers and families stayed before they found accommodations.

I went to wash my face before bed and discovered that there was no running water in the faucet. We learned the next day that the water came on at 6:30 in the morning and would last until about 6:30 in the evening.

At least that was the wintertime arrangement, but as the summer season approached he water was turned off all over town earlier and earlier. By late summer the water was only on in our apartment two hours every other day, some time. There was no guarantee of the time the water would be on. We would leave our kitchen sink faucet turned on so that when the water arrived we would drop everything and run collect water ad do the cleaning cooking, and washing before the water was gone again.

We quickly learned that having our own storage of water was a very good idea. Soon we learned to keep out bathtub filled with water and several large containers, too. We even found a large, copper kettle for sale in the bazaar and brought it home to fill with water. We were very happy to have those pots filled with water.

Today's lesson tells us about the first miracle that Jesus did in public, changing the water into wine at a wedding in Cana. Jesus used very large, empty, stone jars to provide a wonderful blessing, changing some 180 gallons of water freshly poured from the local well into the finest quality wine for the wedding guests.

Today in our world we don 't have to worry about having running water in our homes. We don't have to worry about storing water for daily use or emergencies. Our lives ware not threatened with shortages; in fact, we can run down to the story for whatever we might need. We do stand, like Jesus' new disciples, watching the goings on as the miracle of changing water into win took place, and like the disciples, we, too, can be filled with faith in Jesus.

The story of the wedding at Cana and the water changing into wine gives us a first glance of what will come in Jesus' ministry. You could think of this story as something of a paradigm for Jesus' entire ministry. First, Jesus takes something old and uses it for a new purpose. Second, Jesus takes what is empty and fills it with abundant blessings. Third, Jesus' signs reveal his glory and builds faith in those who witness them.

Weddings don't happen every day for us. They are special times. People over the centuries and across the world have spent great resources for the launching of two young people into the world of marriage. The Jews of Jesus' time were no exception. The wedding ceremony was a great community event. The plans were made to include food, wine, dancing, and entertainment that would last for a week, sometimes longer. The ceremony itself was not long, but the festivities, the music, the dancing filled the time with merriment One of the events that guest looked forward to was when the bride and groom were each placed on wooden chairs and then held high and waltzed and twirled around to happy music.

Everyone would look on the soon-to-be honeymooners and cheer the happy couple.

Our lesson begins with a wedding in which Mary, the mother of Jesus, is involved. Some scholars think that the wedding was for Mary's sister's son. The wedding took place in Cana, a little town several miles north of Nazareth. Jesus and his first five disciples had been included in the wedding celebration. They were all at the house in Cana for the wedding, For all the preparations, though, somehow the wine for this wedding celebration had run out. The wedding party had been going on for a while, but it was far from over, and wine was expected to be available for the duration of the feast.

Mary recognized that the groom was about to be very embarrassed on his important day, because wine would be called for, and there was no more to be had. What could be done?

Mary wasn't overly concerned; her son was there. Jesus would know what to do. This was not the first time that Mary had turned to Jesus to provide something in a pinch.

Mary must have had good reasons to believe, to trust, that Jesus would be able to make things right. She had confidence that turning to

Jesus was the best possible answer. (It is my person belief that Mary must have seen Jesus act in unexpected ways during his growing up years, ways that gave her the confidence to believe that he could rescue this bridegroom's reputation by doing something to fix the scene.

Mary spoke to her son, mentioning the groom's impending embarrassment, the lack of wine was about to be discovered. Jesus' response was almost surprising, *"My time is not yet here, what is this to you or me?"*

In these several words, Jesus tells us that he and his mother understood one another, that they both knew that He was able to do something to help, and that Jesus' actions were directed by His Heavenly Father, who set the time for him to act.

Mary's trust in her son did not waiver. She spoke to the servants say, *"Do whatever my son tells you to do."*

Jesus looked about the yard and spied six stone jars, the sort that were used for ritual washing.

John tells us that these pots were big enough to hold 20-30- gallons of water each.

Jesus told the servants to fill these jars with water. The servants filled them to their brims.

Then Jesus told the servant to di from these newly filled jars and to take the dipper to the chief steward at the wedding.

The servants followed Jesus' bidding, and when the steward tasted from the cup, he was greatly surprised. The water was water no more! The water had become wine! The steward didn't know the source of this new wine, but the servants knew that they had just drawn the water from the well and filled the jars themselves. They knew it was water to begin with.

The chief steward immediately called the groom aside and praised him, saying, *"At other weddings the best wine is always served first, and only later, after everyone's palate has been diminished, then the cheaper wine is given, but you have save the best for now!"*

When I used to read this story about the water turning into wine, I would wonder why the jars were empty to begin with? These jars had a purpose. They were filled with water for the purification rituals observed by the Jews. Those rituals included the washing of dusty, sometimes muddy feet of guests, as well as water for the washing of hands before and during the meals. These customs had been around for hundreds of years. The jars had been used already and were now empty.

Jesus used these old stone jars, which had been used for so long for one purpose, the satisfying of the legal requirement, and He put them to a new use.

When the water was dipped out and give to the head steward of the wedding to taste, the water had become the most wonderful wine! The jars didn't contain water any longer. Jesus took something old and called it to be something new. Later in John we hear how Jesus would use the staff with the bronze serpent to point to his own cross, which would give life to those who look upon it. He also took the bread and wine from the Passover meal and instituted the Lord's Supper from them. Jesus took the towel and bowl of the household slave and made them the sign of our servanthood to the world. Jesus used examples from everyday life to point to the kingdom – the lost is found, entire estates are sold to buy the one treasure of great value, hundreds, probably thousands of people's live were changed by Jesus' healing touch, giving them a whole new life to live.

John tells us that these stone jars were big; they could each hold 20-30 gallons of water in them.

With six jars that means that Jesus made some 150, possibly even 180, gallons of wine that day! You could call that an abundant amount of wine! That's a lot more wine than was needed at that wedding in that village. Jesus provided for the needs of the wedding celebrants and much more. Later in Jesus' ministry he broke five little barley loaves and provided a meal for 5000 men plus women and children, and afterwards the disciples collected twelve baskets full of scraps. Jesus also directed the disciples as they were fishing to find fish in great abundance. Jesus' gift of wine was lavish.

It speaks of the joy and fun and thrill of the wedding itself. It was a time to enjoy and a time to celebrate and make merry. John tells us that this moment was very special. When Jesus turned all that water into fine wine something happened to the day. It changed the day from an ordinary day into one no one would forget.

That day Jesus did something that had never been done before. That day in the presence of many observers a miracle happened. That day Jesus revealed something about himself that others had not before seen or even imagined That day they saw the first sign that Jesus gave providing a glimpse of who he was and is. This first sign was also a sign for other signs to come. The disciples, who would continue to be with Jesus, were now alerted to watch this man, pay attention to him. This first sign was also a first peek at Jesus' glory.

This lesson only briefly mentions Jesus' disciples. There were five disciples. There were very new at being disciples. They had just met the teacher a few days before and had begun traveling with him. They came with Jesus to the wedding festivities and were there, watching on, as the events of this first miracle took place.

That must have been an amazing day for the disciples. The head steward didn't know the source of the wine; the bridegroom didn't know the source of the wine, but the servants did, and the disciples knew.

The disciples grew in their faith that day. They, too, were filled by Jesus. There were filled with faith in him. The could ever return to thinking of Jesus as an ordinary man.

You could say that the disciples were like the stone jars before Jesus called them to follow. The had been fishermen, but Jesus gave them new lives, as fishers of men. They were filled with faith as they walked with their new master.

Jesus told the disciples and us that He came to give us life and to give it abundantly. We can be filled with His love and life, filled abundantly, when we let Jesus into our lives. Jesus has come to celebrate the nuptial feast of a family friend and already the world is beginning to change by His presence.

The old becomes new. The empty becomes abundantly filled, and the glory of the LORD is revealed to all people.

Might we, also, be old jars that can be used for a new purpose?

John 2: 13-25 NIV

13 When it was almost time for the Jewish Passover, Jesus went up to Jerusalem. 14 In the temple courts he found people selling cattle, sheep and doves, and others sitting at tables exchanging money. 15 So he made a whip out of cords, and drove all from the temple courts, both sheep and cattle; he scattered the coins of the money changers and overturned their tables. 16 To those who sold doves he said, "Get these out of here! Stop turning my Father's house into a market!" 17 His disciples remembered that it is written: "Zeal for your house will consume me."[a]

18 The Jews then responded to him, "What sign can you show us to prove your authority to do all this?"

19 Jesus answered them, "Destroy this temple, and I will raise it again in three days."

20 They replied, "It has taken forty-six years to build this temple, and you are going to raise it in three days?" 21 But the temple he had spoken of was his body. 22 After he was raised from the

dead, his disciples recalled what he had said. Then they believed the scripture and the words that Jesus had spoken.

23 Now while he was in Jerusalem at the Passover Festival, many people saw the signs he was performing and believed in his name.[b] 24 But Jesus would not entrust himself to them, for he knew all people. 25 He did not need any testimony about mankind, for he knew what was in each person.

A SIGN FOR ALL TIMES

I think from the day we are born we begin to interpret signs. Even before we can speak we learn to recognize signs and respond to them. Light in the room means time to wake up; that feeling inside means it's time to eat. Signs seem to be changes or indications of something happening or about to happen.

Jesus said that we are good at interpreting signs around us. When we see the first budding of the tree, we now that spring is on its way. When we see the clouds darkening and gathering we can expect a storm. There are signs all around us.

Advertisers are expert in signage. They study how people receive and process signs, and they work to motivate us by their signs.

- Buy this or that
- Go here
- stay there
- eat this
- don't eat that

We see signs in so many places that we're getting pretty good at ignoring them, same way we filter out sounds that we don't want to hear. Signs can be good, and signs can be bad.

Sometimes we are the first ones to notice a sign. A sign might come from conversation we have with others or from some news we get in the mail. But the sign might be an indicator that something is about to happen. We might become aware of something new or different is taking place in our own bodies, which leave us thoughtful and wondering what the 'sign' meant.

Several years ago I visited a man at Sibley Memorial Hospital during my regular rounds as a chaplain. When I looked in on Stan, he shocked me because he looked just like another man I knew, a man who was not easy to like.

It became apparent rather quickly that Stan was not an agreeable person, either. In fact, he growled at me. I didn't spend much time with Stan that morning, but I did learn that he was HIV positive and had been for nine years. He'd also been in and out of the hospital a number of times; this trip was just a routine one. I also learned that Stan was a very successful interior designer in Washington, D.C.

About a week later I discovered that Stan had returned to the hospital, so I looked in on him again. Stan still wore his gruff exterior, but something was different this time. He invited me to sit and talk. As we spoke, it came out that something had happened to Stan the night before. It seems that he had stepped out of bed for a minute, but his legs would not support him, and he collapsed in a heap on the floor! Before that moment Stan had no idea that he was seriously ill. Suddenly he had come face to face with the fact that he might not live much longer; he might have just taken the first step of his last days on earth. Stan was shaken to his core. Something had happened that was a sign, a sign that showed Stan that he was in big trouble!

The Jews in Jerusalem wanted a sign. They asked Jesus for a sign.

They had just witnessed Jesus in the Temple angrily trashing the money boxes, cracking a whip at the merchants, telling them to get out of his Father's House and to take those animals with them!"

The Jews were shocked at Jesus' actions. They could not understand how anyone would think he had the authority to make such a mess.

Jesus had disrupted the commerce and the usual flow of business at the Temple.

The Jews asked for a sign. "What sign can you give us that will explain your actions?"

When Jesus answered their question, nobody understood what he said, but this morning we can be Monday morning quarterbacks with nearly 2000 years of history behind us. We will be able to see more clearly what the Jews and the disciples could not see that day.

We can look at the sign that Jesus told about and marvel at it. We can look at the sign that Jesus foretold and know it is <u>A Sign for All Times</u>.

One of the wonders of the Mid-East is their bazaars. I expect every middle-sized or large city in the Mid-East has a bazaar. Bazaars are places where the vendors of everything you would ever need sell their wares.

If you need bread or fish or veggies

If you need kitchenware or bedding or carpet

If you need shoes or clothes or yardage

If you need furnishings of any kind

If you need a bite to eat or 24 carat gold bracelets or meerschaum pipes

You can find it at the bazaar.

Bazaars are made up primarily of vendors with pushcarts, standing under large canopies. There are some actual streets, walking streets, on which more permanent businesses stand. The jewelry vendors are all on a very long street. Each has a large window in front with tall stacks of gold bracelets standing high and blazing gold from very bright lights.

It is quite easy to get lost in a bazaar. When Dave and I would visit Konak, the bazaar in Izmir, we quickly learned to add an extra hour to the trip for getting lost and then found again.

Two things you could count on at the bazaar— noise and smell. Both were strong. The smell came from the fish. The noise came from everywhere. Such is a market place in the Mid-East. It would be hard to get tired of such a place, but it is hardly a place where you could find peace or a moment to pray.

The Temple in Jerusalem was a very large building, really a series of buildings. It consisted of the Temple itself and was surrounded by outer courts, concentrically placed. The outside court was open to Gentiles. Anyone could come there. Inside it was the court of the women. The Jewish women were allowed to enter there, but they could go no further. Inside the women's court lay the court of the men, where all Jewish men were permitted to come. Finally, came the sacred Temple area where the priests officiated, where offerings were made daily for the people.

Every Jewish man was responsible to pay a yearly Temple tax that was about two day's wages. This tax had to be made in coinage that could be paid in the Temple. Many coins of the day bore the image of some king or the Emperor, making it unacceptable to be used in the Temple. So money-changers were necessary to get the right coins for the tax.

People came to Jerusalem during the Holy Days of Passover to give offerings and sacrifices in the Temple. They needed to buy animals-- birds, sheep, and cattle for the sacrifices. So many animal vendors with their victims kept shop in the court of the Gentiles.

When Jesus arrived at the Temple, he entered first into the court of the Gentiles. That was where all the commotion was happening. Mind you, there was not a full-fledged bazaar in the Temple. The fish were missing and many businesses, but St. John tells us that the atmosphere and the sounds around the temple very much resembled a market place.

When Jesus saw that many vendors and merchants had moved into the Temple and how it had changed from being a house of prayer to something resembling the bazaar, he acted. He fashioned a whip from some cords and began to drive the animals out of the Temple. Then he overturned the tables of the moneychangers, tossing coins everywhere. He yelled at those selling birds, "Remove these creatures at once; stop making my Father's house a place of commerce!"

It must have been shocking, seeing this man from Galilee angrily throwing tables over, scattering coins all around, snapping a whip at animals to move them toward the gate. Jesus was everywhere at once, it seemed. People didn't expect any such disruptions and were amazed at it.

The Jews didn't know how to respond. Clearly this man had a purpose in his actions. He was not actually harming any persons, he was just trying to remove them from the Temple. But why was he doing this? And, better yet, who gave him the authority to do it?

After things had settled down a bit, some of the Jews approached Jesus and asked him to explain himself. They asked, "What sign can you show us for doing this?" The Jews wanted some sort of proof of authority from Jesus. They knew that prophets of old occasionally did bizarre things to bring God's message to the people. The prophets had authority from on high.

Jesus answered them, but the Jews didn't understand; neither did Jesus' disciples understand him.

Jesus said, "Destroy this Temple and in three days I will build it up."

Three days? What was he talking about? There is no way anyone could rebuild the Temple in three days. It had taken Herod forty-six years to get it built so far, and it was not yet complete.

The Jews walked away shaking their heads. Was Jesus out of his mind? What would cause someone to act and speak so strangely?

John tells us that it wasn't until later that the disciples remembered Jesus' words that day and realized what he meant by them.

What was this sign Jesus spoke of?

In the Synoptic Gospels we hear about the sign. It is the same sign, but it is not obvious that it is the same. You have to think about it.

Both Matthew and Luke write about a time when Jesus was asked for a sign for the people.

In those stories Jesus said there would be no sign except for one, the sign of Jonah … the sign of Jonah?

We remember the story of Jonah from our time in Sunday school. Jonah was the man God told to go to Nineveh to prophecy to the people there and tell them to repent. Jonah didn't want to go to Nineveh. He knew how terrible the Assyrian people were, and he also knew that if they repented God would be merciful on them. So Jonah ran away, actually he sailed away. He got on a ship headed into the Mediterranean to get as far away from where God wanted him to go as possible.

The ship Jonah took ran into a terrible storm, and the ship was nearly lost. Jonah knew he was to blame for the storm, because he had disobeyed God, so he told his shipmates to throw him overboard. They did. A great fish came by and swallowed Jonah whole and took him to safety. When Jonah was finally back on land, he went to Nineveh and prophesied, calling the people to repentance.

Did you see the sign in the story? Did you see the sign Jesus was talking about?

"Destroy this temple and in three days I will raise it up". Jonah lived in the belly of the great fish for three days before he was delivered to the safety of the shore.

Three days. That was the sign Jesus was talking about. He would be in the belly of the earth for three days, and then he would rise. He would rise from the dead.

The sign is all about Jesus' death and resurrection. His answer to the Jews was that they would destroy the temple, his body, the temple of God, and on the third day he would rise and live again.

What a sign! If that would happen, it would be the only time in the history of humankind that any person has ever been resurrected.

The sign Jesus foretold was the perfect answer to the Jew's question of authority. His resurrection from the dead showed the world Jesus' authority. He had been approved by his Father in Heaven; his resurrection showed us that.

When Jesus met the eleven disciples on the mount in Galilee just before he ascended into Heaven, he greeted them with these words, "All authority, in heaven and on earth, has been given to me."

Jesus had the authority that the Jews were asking about.

We can understand what Jesus meant by the sign he foretold, but how is that a Sign for All Time? How is Jesus' sign something important for us today?

The sign is that Jesus would rise from the dead. We celebrate Jesus' sign because it spells out resurrection for us. In Jesus we have new life, new possibilities. Even when we find that our lives have been badly messed up, we can find help and hope and new beginnings in Jesus. Jesus' sign is the Sign for All Times.

Remember Stan, the fellow I mentioned earlier, the one who had experienced a sign about his own life, that he could be facing the end?

That day Stan and I talked for some time about the scare he had had. As we talked about his collapse the night before, it became apparent that he was in real pain, not physical, but emotional pain. He was facing the possibility that he wasn't going to live any longer, and terror gripped him.

After a bit I asked Stan if he would like to pray with me, and he agreed. I asked to hold his hand and he gave me his. Then we prayed together.

It was a simple prayer.

I thanked God for his love and care for Stan, for Stan's friends, his love for art and beauty, his opportunities to travel. I recognized the pain, terror, hurt, scare he was feeling. I asked the LORD to reach out and touch him---let him feel His presence. I asked for care by the medical staff. I prayed in Jesus' name and said, "Amen."

After we prayed, both our eyes were wet with tears. I squeezed Stan's hand and he squeezed mine back. I don't know what happened to Stan that day, but I felt that he had come to terms with some things. I felt a real closeness to him that I would not have thought possible earlier. I had a feeling that a miracle was happening right then.

I never saw Stan again. I don't know what happened to him or where he is right now. But I believe that the sign that he had, when he collapsed on the floor, was maybe the best thing that ever happened to him, because it gave him the opportunity to consider what Jesus' sign meant to him—that is, what Jesus meant to Stan. The sign may have started Stan making some important changes in his life. That day in the hospital room we were clearly on Holy Ground.

Jesus' sign is a sign for all of us and A Sign for All Times. Jesus' sign is the sign of the cross. In fact it's the empty cross, because it shows that he rose. The cross reminds us immediately that Jesus suffered and died on that horrible tree, but he also rose. He is not still on the cross, suffering, but he went to the cross for us, for our sins, so that we can be re-established with the Father as God's children.

Jesus' sign is a Sign for All Times because Jesus' sign is a symbol of who Jesus is and what he did for us and continues to do for us every day.

Jesus' sign is a Sign for All Times. It is there to remind us that the signs that we receive every day—good signs and bad signs—are not all there is for us. Jesus' sign is there to call us to come to Him: to follow him; to trust Him to be with us and act for us as we move through each day.

It is my prayer for each of us, that when we see signs that indicate changes or opportunities or troubles in our lives, we also look immediately to Jesus' sign and remember how those worldly signs are not the final word. The signs we see every day will pass away, but God's love for us in Christ will never pass away. Amen.

John 3: 1-17

3 Now there was a Pharisee, a man named Nicodemus who was a member of the Jewish ruling council. 2 He came to Jesus at night and said, "Rabbi, we know that you are a teacher who has come from God. For no one could perform the signs you are doing if God were not with him."

3 Jesus replied, "Very truly I tell you, no one can see the kingdom of God unless they are born again.[a]"

4 "How can someone be born when they are old?" Nicodemus asked. "Surely they cannot enter a second time into their mother's womb to be born!"

5 Jesus answered, "Very truly I tell you, no one can enter the kingdom of God unless they are born of water and the Spirit. 6 Flesh gives birth to flesh, but the Spirit[b] gives birth to spirit. 7 You should not be surprised at my saying, 'You[c] must be born again.' 8 The wind blows wherever it pleases. You hear its sound, but you cannot tell where it comes from or where it is going. So it is with everyone born of the Spirit."[d]

9 "How can this be?" Nicodemus asked.

¹⁰ "You are Israel's teacher," said Jesus, "and do you not understand these things? ¹¹ Very truly I tell you, we speak of what we know, and we testify to what we have seen, but still you people do not accept our testimony. ¹² I have spoken to you of earthly things and you do not believe; how then will you believe if I speak of heavenly things? ¹³ No one has ever gone into heaven except the one who came from heaven—the Son of Man.[e] ¹⁴ Just as Moses lifted up the snake in the wilderness, so the Son of Man must be lifted up,[f] ¹⁵ that everyone who believes may have eternal life in him."[g]

¹⁶ For God so loved the world that he gave his one and only Son, that whoever believes in him shall not perish but have eternal life. ¹⁷ For God did not send his Son into the world to condemn the world, but to save the world through him.

MINE! EVEN MINE!

…whosoever believeth in him should not perish, but have everlasting life.'

There's a story in the book of Numbers that some of you won't remember. It tells of the Israelites wandering in the desert. They have been there for a while, and they're not happy with things. They have complained before, and they received water and manna and quail, so they had something to eat and drink, but they were not happy. They continued wandering, and they continued complaining. Their memories told them that things had been better back in Egypt when they had been slaves, so they murmured against God and Moses.

Then God sent many poisonous snakes to the land, and many of the people died from their venom. So then they complained to Moses about the snakes saying *'We have sinned by speaking against the LORD and against you; pray to the LORD to take away the serpents from us.'* (Num 21: 6) Then God told Moses to make a bronze serpent and put it on the end of his staff and raise up the staff so that all the people could gaze on it. When someone was bitten, he or she could look up at the bronze snake and be healed; he or she would not die.

That's quite a colorful story, but it's a really strange thing that God told Moses to do—to fashion a serpent, put it on a pole, and hold it up for everyone to see.

Jesus mentions this story of the bronze serpent to Nicodemus, the Pharisee, when he called on Jesus one night. Nicodemus told Jesus he knew that Jesus must have come from God, because of all the good things Jesus was doing. And Jesus told Nicodemus that he needed to be born again.

Nicodemus failed to understand what Jesus meant by being born again, so Jesus pointed to that event in the desert long time back when the Israelites were dying because of the many poisonous snakes, and God told Moses to make a serpent, affix it to the stick, and hold it up in the air for all to see. Anyone who was bitten by a snake could look on the bronze serpent and live.

As I was thinking about that scene in the wilderness and Moses and the snake, I wondered why it was that God told Moses to make a snake for the people. What was it about a snake that would be significant? Why didn't God tell Moses to make an apple or a tree or some other animal? How about a duplicate of the Ten Commandments? What was it about the snake that was important? Or maybe it didn't matter.

Then I remembered the serpent in the garden. We know that story well—Adam and Eve in the garden. The serpent had insinuated itself into the garden and into Miss Eve's presence.

We remember how the serpent deceived Eve with a promise of knowledge. He said, *'You will not die; for God knows that when you eat of [the fruit of the tree in the middle of the garden] your eyes will be opened, and you will be like God, knowing good and evil.'* (Gen 3:4-5)

The serpent's conversation with Eve caused the First Couple to disobey God's command about not eating the fruit. When they did eat it, their eyes were opened, and they realized they were naked, and they were no longer in the same, comfortable position with God that they had enjoyed before.

The serpent had enticed them to disobey God's command, and they fell. They were now enemies of God!

It was the serpents that brought death to those wandering in the wilderness. Moses sought God's help and God told Moses to make the serpent and hold it upon the stick for all to see. The snake which brought death to them was now bringing health and restoration and life.

Fast-forward to John's gospel and Jesus and Nicodemus. Jesus was trying to explain to the Pharisee what Jesus was about to do, and he reached back into the history of the Israelites to that moment in time with Moses and the Israelites and the serpents. Jesus used the picture that he knew Nicodemus knew, for he was a teacher of the faith.

Jesus said, '*And just as Moses lifted up the serpent in the wilderness, so must the Son of Man be lifted up, that whosoever believes in him may have eternal life.*' (John 3:14-15)

The bronze snake represented the serpents that were killing the Israelites. It was just like those deadly snakes that were everywhere killing the people. They were dying until they looked on the bronze serpent, the one raised up, and when they looked on it, they stopped dying. They were healed of their snake bites.

Jesus was telling Nicodemus that the Son of Man would be like the bronze snake. He would be the one who would take on the sins of the world. (People are dying because of their sin-- what happened in the garden--and Jesus would take their sin on himself.) When Jesus died, he did not die as one without sin, although he had been sinless before he arrived at Golgotha. He took on the sin of the world as he hung there on the cross; he carried all the sin of the world in himself. He died with all those sins. He took them to their death.

Anyone who looks on Jesus will live because of his sacrifice.

Jesus took on the sin of the world when he died on the cross, and his death is the salvation of all who look to him for healing.

I guess I hadn't really thought about it before, that Jesus' taking on the sin of the world when he died at Calvary was like the bronze serpent in the wilderness. The people who were afflicted by the snake bites were healed when they looked upon the bronze serpent. That is the picture Jesus wanted Nicodemus to remember and to understand about what Jesus would soon be doing.

Keep this in mind as we move into the rest of the scripture lesson.

'For God so loved the world that he gave his only Son, so that everyone who believes in him may not perish but may have eternal life.' (3:16)

Those words may be some of the best known words in the Bible—

for God so loved the world that he gave his only begotten Son, that whosoever believeth in Him may not perish, but have everlasting life.

God so loved the world ... God created our world and made it good, like all that God makes.

God so loved the world ... that God sent the Son.

I actually think that God planned all along to send the Son into the world to be incarnate in this world, which means that He connects the world with God. In Christ we have the *complete connection of God and creation. Whatever happens to Christ happens to creation.*

God so loved the world ... God created our world, and it is good, like all that God makes. God so loved the world ... that God sent the Son.

God so loved the world, that he sent his only Begotten Son.

God sent the Son into the world to save us. I have to believe that God knew from before the beginning that the creatures made in God's image would fail and be at enmity to God. Yet IN SPITE of this failure, God sent the Son. God so loved the world that God sent the Son to become the salvation of all who look to him.

God so loved the world that he gave his only Begotten Son, so that whosoever believeth in him.

God sent the Son to take on the sins of the world, to take them to the cross and die with them. So that whosoever believes in him…

Believing in Jesus the Christ is first looking to him—turning to him, trusting him.

Like those who had been bitten in the wilderness by the deadly poisonous snakes, we, too, are dying in our sin, before we look to Jesus. We haven't been bitten by a poisonous snake, but we are dying nonetheless from our sins. We need a redeemer. One who is able to take away our sin.

God so loved the world, that he sent his only begotten son, that whosoever believeth…

That WHOSOEVER is important. Whosoever means anyone who … Anyone who believes. It doesn't matter your age, your sex, your color, your station in life, or any other distinction, when you believe in Jesus you benefit from his sacrifice.

I like Jesus' words we read in St. Matthew, when Jesus was instituting the LORD's Supper, and he took the cup, and gave thanks over it and gave it to his disciples to drink, saying, 'this is my blood of the covenant, which is poured out for many for the forgiveness of sins.

Jesus said his blood was about to be poured out for many for the forgiveness of sins. Some people would rather hear the word 'all' instead of 'many', but I like the word many, because it indicates that each person for whom Jesus poured out his blood was an individual, one of many, but still an individual. Poured out for many. That means for you and for me.

Whosoever believeth in him…

Almost three centuries ago a young Anglican priest was in a terrible state. John Wesley, the priest, was well educated. He had been to Oxford and flourished as an academic there. He took holy orders and became a priest. He understood a lot about faith in Christ. He came from parents who were strong Christian leaders. His father, Samuel Wesley, was an Anglican priest. His mother, Suzanna, came from a long history of Non-Conformist Protestants. Wesley learned about faith in Jesus from them.

But I wonder if Wesley had not missed a critical detail in his early training?

You see, when he went to the Moravian Bible study at the church on Aldersgate Street one evening in May in 1738, he was not a happy man. He had just returned from a year in Savannah, Georgia, where he had had much difficulty.

He returned to London after a year, depressed and frustrated. One evening he wrote in his Journal these words. "In the evening I went very unwillingly to a society in Aldersgate Street, where one was reading Luther's preface to the Epistle to the Romans. About a quarter before nine, while the leader was describing the change which God works in the heart through faith in Christ, I felt my heart strangely warmed. I felt I did trust in Christ alone for salvation; and an assurance was given me that He had taken away my sins, even mine, and saved me from the law of sin and death."

Do you see it? It sounds like at that moment Wesley finally recognized Christ's work on the cross for him personally. He no longer was using the faith of his parents or his teachers, he owned it himself: *'I was given assurance that Christ had taken away my sins, even mine, and saved me from the law of sin and death.'*

Isn't that what each of us needs to have? We need to have faith ourselves and not the faith of someone else. We can't lean on someone else's faith forever. We need to come to the saving knowledge of Christ being our redeemer. He, personally, is our savior.

Each of us must look on the cross and know that Jesus took our sin and died for each of us. It is not enough for us to rely on the faith of our fathers or our mothers or someone else we admire. We need to know that the faith we have is faith that has our names on it.

We need to be able to say, "I trust in Christ alone for salvation; I know that He has taken away my sins, even mine, and had saved me from the law of sin and death.

John 3:1-17
Ephesians 2:8.

FAITH THAT SAVES

There's an old, not very funny, joke about a man who was sent to prison. The first day when he went to the cafeteria for lunch he noticed that as all the inmates sat eating their meal, every so often one man would rise up from his chair and say in a loud voice some number ... (10, 78, 34 and so on) and then everyone would laugh ... a big hearty-har-har. This happened several times during lunch and the man was really wondering what he had witnessed.

So he asked his roommate later that day. What in the world did those numbers mean? The roommate told the man, "Oh, those numbers each stand for a joke, but we don't have time when we eat to tell an entire joke so we've numbered the jokes and when someone stands up and recites a number, we think of the joke and the punch line, and then we all laugh at the joke. It saves time."

"Aha!", thought the man. So the next time the inmates were all gathered for a meal the new man stood up and called out a number, one he had heard called out before. After he called out the number, he sat down waiting the expected response, but no one laughed. "Hm", he thought, so after he'd finished eating, he stood up and hollered out another number, but he got the same response, nothing.

The man wondered why his 'joke telling' hadn't resulted in any laughter, so he asked his roomie what he thought had gone wrong. "Oh, the roommate answered, "I think some people can tell 'em and some just can't."

Okay, that's not the funniest joke, but I think it does point out an interesting fact about us Christians. I think that we have some of those 'inside' jokes (or really scriptures) that we refer to by the number—the 23d Psalm-for instance. And we all know what we're talking about. Of course, the average man on the street has no idea what we're talking about,

I heard about some man who showed up at the Super Bowl, wearing a T-shirt with the words: John 3:16 printed in large letters on his back. He likes to get in front of the camera at the super bowl. It's his way of witnessing his faith to a large audience—everyone who's tuned in to watch the Super Bowl that day will see the man and his 'ad' on his back.

I believe that Americans these days are not well versed in Bible and might not know what the number John 3:16 means. In fact not a great percentage of Americans can even recite the names of the four gospel writers—Matthew, Mark, Luke, and John.

I think that some of us who have known John 3:16 … forever, sort of think that it's the gospel in a nutshell. It's the whole thing wrapped up in a few words. If we know it … then we're saved.

John three: sixteen is a wonderful verse, but it's really a message that needs to be unpacked. That's what I hope we can do this morning. Hopefully we will know not just the number— John 3:16, but we'll know the whole story, too.

Read Scripture John 3: 1-17

So there was Nicodemus, a Pharisee, who came to visit the LORD under the cover of darkness.

Now Pharisees were teachers of the Law, not only teachers but practitioners of the Law. They had vowed to live completely by the Law, which meant they lived a very prescribed life.

Jesus often faults the Pharisees as being 'pretty' on the outside but decaying on the inside. Their lives from the outside were something to look at. They were the ones that others looked up to see how to be just exactly right according to the Law.

Jesus said the lives of Pharisees were all for show to others, but God, who looks on the heart, saw something quite different. Pharisees lived in the present and the literal meaning of life. They thought that by following the Law fastidiously they would gain eternal life. Pharisees also believed in the resurrection.

When Nicodemus met Jesus he told him that Jesus must be close to God, in fact he must have come from God, because of all the miraculous signs that Jesus had done. Jesus' signs told everyone that God was clearly with Jesus.

Jesus answered Nicodemus, saying that if one would see the Kingdom of God, it must come through a new birth, a birth from above.

Nicodemus' answer to Jesus is almost funny. He asked, *"What am I to climb back into my mother's womb and be born again? How might one go about doing that?* (There's that literal, looking for a loop hole logic.)

Jesus repeated his earlier statement and went a bit further this time. He said, "If anyone wants to see the Kingdom of God he must be born a second time of water and the Spirit. Jesus was telling Nicodemus that this birth would include baptism (water) and the Holy Spirit, which invades our hearts and quickens us to new life in Christ.

When we read John's Gospel we have to understand that John was written differently than the first three evangelists. Matthew, Mark, and Luke wrote a chronological account of Jesus' life in ministry, death, and resurrection. But St. John had a different purpose in writing. His objective was more theological. John wrote to tell his readers, and us, that Jesus was the Christ, the Son of God, and that believing, we would have eternal life. (John 20:31)

That's what John also says in John 3:16 ... *That whosoever believes in [Jesus] will have eternal life.*

 But there are many ways of believing. It may not be every way of believing in Jesus that ends up with eternal life.

You'll have to agree that we may know folks who say they are Christian, who have some church experience, whose family was connected to some church, but they don't darken the doors of a church these days. And we have to ask, "Are these 'believers' on the way to the Kingdom that Jesus came to inaugurate?

How can I know?

John Wesley wrote about that very thing. In his First Sermon, Salvation by Faith, Wesley asked that very question. "What is the faith that saves?" And then Wesley answered his own question by citing four different types of people and their faith.

First, Wesley says, it is NOT the faith of the heathens, in other words, it is not the 'culturally Christian world." (For instance we live in America, and our country is considered to be 'culturally Christian". (I suppose you could say that just because one is born in America, one is not automatically a Christian, any more than just because you are standing in a garage, doesn't mean that you are a FORD Mustang!)

Wesley says that God still requires that the Heathens believe:

- First that God exists
- That God is a rewarder of them that diligently seek him
- That God is to be sought by glorifying him as God
- By giving thanks for all things
- By a careful practice of moral virtue of justice, mercy, and truth, toward our fellow creatures.

Wesley says that a Greek or a Roman ... yea, even a Scythian or an Indian (and couldn't we add many other cultures to that list today?) are without excuse if they do not believe as much. (This comes from St. Paul's letter to the Romans, Chapter One, when Paul says the same. Creation itself clearly tells of God's handiwork. Anyone who sees and experiences anything of creation is without excuse if he does not believe.

"Ever since the creation of the world [God's] eternal power and divine nature, invisible though they are, have been understood and seen through the things he has made. So [wicked people] are without excuse."

They also must believe in the being and attributes of God

- A future state of reward and punishment
- And the obligatory nature of moral value.

Second, Wesley points to the devil. He says that the Faith that Saves is not the faith of the devil.

The Bible tells us that devils believe not only that there is a wise and powerful God, Gracious to reward and just to punish, but also that Jesus is the Son of God, The Christ, the Savior of the World.

Remember the demon who said, "I know thee, who thou art, the Holy One of God?"

The great enemy of God and man believes and trembles in believing that God was made manifest in the flesh, that he will 'tread all enemies under his feet," and that 'all scripture was given by inspiration of God."

Thus far is the faith of a devil. It is not a faith that will save.

Nor is the faith of the Apostles, themselves, which they had while Christ was yet upon the earth. Though they so believed on him as to 'leave all and follow him." E'en though they had then the power to work miracles to 'heal al manner of sickness and all manner of disease."

They even had the 'power and authority over all devils'. And more than this, they were sent by the Master to "preach the Kingdom of

God." Even the faith of the Apostles was not faith that saves.

What then is the faith that saves? Which Paul speaks of in Ephesians 2:8: By Grace we are saved through faith?

First it is faith in Christ. Before anything else we must believe in Christ and God's action in Christ. Jesus did not come alone to this world to save it. He came from the Father. The plan had been there from the beginning. Christ would come into the world and inaugurate the Kingdom and make a way for creation to come into the Kingdom.

God was working through Christ. As Nicodemus said, "You must have come from God, for no one can do the things you do without coming from God."

Our fiath must not be some rational argument or lifeless philosophy; our faith must come from our heart, not only head knowledge.

Remember the words of St. Paul written to the Christians in Rome? "With the heart a man believes unto Righteousness, and "If thou shall confess with thy mouth the Lord Jesus, and shall believe with thy heart that God hath raised him from the dead, thou shall be saved. (Rom 10:9)

Second: The faith that saves recognizes that Jesus had to die. Jesus' death was necessary. The faith that saves recognized that there was merit in Jesus' death. Even the Apostles' faith, as much as they had seen and experienced from Jesus before the passion was not a saving faith. They had yet to see Christ's suffering, death, and resurrection.

The faith that saves recognizes the merit in Jesus' death. His death was not meaningless; it had the greatest meaning of all. Jesus' death satisfied God's requirements to bring humans back into fellowship with God. Jesus' sacrifice was the only way reconciliation could happen.

Third: A faith that saves recognizes the power of Jesus' Resurrection.

The resurrection tells us that we are saved and have eternal life.

Do you remember Jesus' words to his disciples when he was at the well in Samaria? "My food is to do the will of the one who sent me and to complete his work." (John 4:34)

Jesus' perfect obedience to his Father's will, submitting to the suffering and death on the cross provides us with the Righteousness necessary to salvation. Therefore there is merit in Christ's death. Believing in the blood of Christ is belief in the merits of his death and resurrection. Trusting in Jesus' blood is another way of saying we have faith in Christ's obedience to God's will, the suffering and death on the cross.

There is nothing within us that merits Heaven, but Jesus offers us the invitation to the Kingdom through his own sacrifice, his own Righteousness.

Grace is the love of God that loves us even though we don't deserve it. It is the love that comes to us through the work of Christ on the cross, the total giving love that God has done for us.

I recently heard a picture of Grace that I'd like to share with you. It was told by a seminary professor at Perkins. I think it may have been a story about himself as a young man:

The professor said that when he was a child he and his mother never shopped at a store that didn't give S & H Green Stamps. The man remembered that it was his job each Friday afternoon to go to the glove compartment of the car and to pull out all the green stamps and to stick the onto the pages of the green stamp books. Then after a couple of months the boy and the mother would collect all the books they had gathered and head off for the redemption center to buy something with those books.

The redemption center had all sorts of wonderful items there. These items were standing on shelves in the front room of the redemption center. On one particular trip, the boy cast his eye high up on a shelf. There he spied a large, beautifully striped stuffed tiger. The boy immediately wanted the tiger; he loved the tiger. He wanted that tiger and begged his mom to get it for him.

"No," the mother said, "We don't have enough stamp books to purchase it today. We'll have to go home and save up more stamp books before we can get that tiger."

The boy anxiously awaited the next trip to the redemption center. Finally the day came, the boy and his mother went to the S & H store, and the tiger was redeemed. The tiger finally belonged to the boy, and he was trilled to have it in his arms.

That's a great picture of redemption. The tiger didn't do anything to be redeemed or to deserve being redeemed. There is no understanding of why the boy wanted that tiger, but the boy loved the tiger and that was enough. He wanted the tiger and he worked to get it.

And the boy didn't just redeem the tiger, he wanted to keep the tiger with him.

Isn't that how it is for us? It's not that we have done anything spectacular to deserve God's love, but he loves us just the same. And He's gone a long way out of his way to redeem us, to have us belong to him, to have us in his company and fellowship.

John 4: 5-42 NIV

5 *So he came to a town in Samaria called Sychar, near the plot of ground Jacob had given to his son Joseph.* 6 *Jacob's well was there, and Jesus, tired as he was from the journey, sat down by the well. It was about noon.*

7 *When a Samaritan woman came to draw water, Jesus said to her, "Will you give me a drink?"* 8 *(His disciples had gone into the town to buy food.)*

9 *The Samaritan woman said to him, "You are a Jew and I am a Samaritan woman. How can you ask me for a drink?" (For Jews do not associate with Samaritans.[a])*

10 *Jesus answered her, "If you knew the gift of God and who it is that asks you for a drink, you would have asked him and he would have given you living water."*

11 *"Sir," the woman said, "you have nothing to draw with and the well is deep. Where can you get this living water?* 12 *Are you greater than our father Jacob, who gave us the well and*

drank from it himself, as did also his sons and his livestock?"

¹³ Jesus answered, "Everyone who drinks this water will be thirsty again,¹⁴ but whoever drinks the water I give them will never thirst. Indeed, the water I give them will become in them a spring of water welling up to eternal life."

¹⁵ The woman said to him, "Sir, give me this water so that I won't get thirsty and have to keep coming here to draw water."

¹⁶ He told her, "Go, call your husband and come back."

¹⁷ "I have no husband," she replied.

Jesus said to her, "You are right when you say you have no husband.¹⁸ The fact is, you have had five husbands, and the man you now have is not your husband. What you have just said is quite true."

¹⁹ "Sir," the woman said, "I can see that you are a prophet. ²⁰ Our ancestors worshiped on this mountain, but you Jews claim that the place where we must worship is in Jerusalem."

21 "Woman," Jesus replied, "believe me, a time is coming when you will worship the Father neither on this mountain nor in Jerusalem. 22 You Samaritans worship what you do not know; we worship what we do know, for salvation is from the Jews. 23 Yet a time is coming and has now come when the true worshipers will worship the Father in the Spirit and in truth, for they are the kind of worshipers the Father seeks. 24 God is spirit, and his worshipers must worship in the Spirit and in truth."

25 The woman said, "I know that Messiah" (called Christ) "is coming. When he comes, he will explain everything to us."

26 Then Jesus declared, "I, the one speaking to you—I am he."

27 Just then his disciples returned and were surprised to find him talking with a woman. But no one asked, "What do you want?" or "Why are you talking with her?"

28 Then, leaving her water jar, the woman went back to the town and said to the people, 29 "Come, see a man who

told me everything I ever did. Could this be the Messiah?" ³⁰ They came out of the town and made their way toward him.

³¹ Meanwhile his disciples urged him, "Rabbi, eat something."

³² But he said to them, "I have food to eat that you know nothing about."

³³ Then his disciples said to each other, "Could someone have brought him food?"

³⁴ "My food," said Jesus, "is to do the will of him who sent me and to finish his work. ³⁵ Don't you have a saying, 'It's still four months until harvest'? I tell you, open your eyes and look at the fields! They are ripe for harvest. ³⁶ Even now the one who reaps draws a wage and harvests a crop for eternal life, so that the sower and the reaper may be glad together. ³⁷ Thus the saying 'One sows and another reaps' is true. ³⁸ I sent you to reap what you have not worked for. Others have done the hard work, and you have reaped the benefits of their labor."

³⁹ Many of the Samaritans from that town believed in him because of the

woman's testimony, "He told me everything I ever did." 40 So when the Samaritans came to him, they urged him to stay with them, and he stayed two days. 41 And because of his words many more became believers.

42 They said to the woman, "We no longer believe just because of what you said; now we have heard for ourselves, and we know that this man really is the Savior of the world."

IN SPIRIT AND IN TRUTH

Jesus and his disciples were on a journey. They had started in Jerusalem, having spent the Passover in the Holy City. Now, they were returning to Galilee. They decided to go through Samaria, an unusual choice, figuring how Jews really didn't enjoy traveling through Samaritan country.

But Jesus had something special in mind. The disciples didn't know about it. Around noon they arrived at a little town called Sychar, where a famous old well was outside the town's gate. The well was the well that Jacob, one of the great patriarch's, had dug.

The disciples left Jesus by the well to rest while they made their way into town in search of a noonday meal.

So ... Jesus was sitting at the well when a woman of the town arrived to draw water. The woman came to the well and put down her bucket and drew out a bucketful of water. Jesus spoke to her. "Woman, give me some water to drink."

The woman was surprised. She didn't know the man who spoke, but she knew from his dress that he was not a Samaritan; he was a Jew.

Jews and Samaritans didn't have business with one another. They lived separate lives. Like ships passing in the night, they ignored each other. Too many times in the past the Samaritans and the Jews had clashed. The Jews felt superior. They were the pure race. The Samaritans were a mix of Israelite and Assyrian blood, and to the Jews that meant they were 'unclean'.

The woman was surprised on another account. She was surprised that this man spoke to her because men and women who were not related never spoke to one another. That was an age-old social understanding. Men and women must not speak to one another unless they were in the same family—father/daughter; husband/wife; brother/sister. A man outside of the family could not speak to a woman on the street, or it would be considered as a proposition, and that was against the law.

But the man had spoken to her. He was not propositioning her; he simply asked for water.

"How is it that you, a Jew, ask me, a Samaritan woman, for water?" she asked.

Jesus looked in her eyes (another social no-no) and said, "If you knew the gift of God and who it is that is saying to you, 'Give me a drink, you would have asked him, and he would have given you living water."

The woman, surprised again, asked, "How is it that you can give me drink? You don't even have a bucket! Where would you get living water? Are you greater than our ancestor Jacob, who gave us the well, and with his sons and flocks drank from it?"

The Samaritans always spoke of the God of Abraham, the God of Isaac, and the God of Jacob. They were great in the minds and hearts of all Israelites. Was this man suggesting that he was equal to them?

Jesus replied, "Everyone who drinks of this water will be thirsty again, but those who drink of the water that I will give them will never be thirsty. The water I will give them will become in them a spring of water gushing up to eternal life."

Jesus was pointing out the difference between physical needs and spiritual needs. We humans live on both of those planes at the same time—physical and spiritual. Both need nourishment.

We are very aware of our physical needs, and we're pretty good about attending to them.

Our spiritual bodies also need nourishment, and that's an area we may be less careful with.

The Samaritan woman was not unlike the Pharisee, Nicodemus. He didn't understand what Jesus was talking about either. Nicodemus reacted when Jesus told him that he needed to be 'born again.' How could he climb back into his mother's womb and be born again? He was thinking only about the physical side of life, but Jesus was referring to our need to be born a second time as a spiritual person.

The woman took Jesus' words literally, thinking that Jesus was talking about water he would take from a well to satisfy her thirst.

Jesus was speaking about giving her Living Water, which would quench her spiritual thirst permanently. 'It would be like a spring of water gushing up for eternity.'

Jesus changed the subject. He told the woman, 'Go back to the village and bring your husband here.'

"I have no husband," she answered.

Jesus said, "You speak the truth. You don't, currently, have a husband. You have had five husbands, and the man you have now is not your husband."

This comment from Jesus usually raises the picture of a wanton woman, one who has divorced many times … searching for the right man.

But we have to remember that back in Jesus' time, women did not divorce husbands. It was the right of the husband to divorce his wife … for whatever reason he found. She might have been a bad cook; she gave him no sons; she didn't please him. The Samaritan woman might have been widowed several times. We can only guess.

And, Jesus noted, "the man you are with now is not your husband."

One of the things about Christian faith is that you never meet Jesus without also learning about yourself. The truth comes out.

The woman was not without sin. It is true. As Paul tells us, 'All have sinned and fallen short of the glory of God.' (Rom 3:23) The woman's life was exposed. There was no hiding her failure. She stood in need of God's grace, just as we all do.

And she was shocked! How could this man, this Jew, whom she hadn't met, know about her life? How could he? Unless … unless he was a prophet. Somehow prophets knew stuff about people, about God, that was hidden from the rest of the world.

(Everyone in her village knew the woman. She may not have been a popular citizen. She may have chosen the mid of the day to come for her daily water, thinking to avoid the gathering of women that met earlier in the morning at the well. She may have wanted to avoid their stares or their cutting remarks.)

"Sir', she said, 'I perceive you are a prophet."

Then she asked, 'You know, our leaders tell us that we should worship on Mt. Gerizim, but you Jews say true worship must be done in Jerusalem. Can you tell me which is right?'[This scripture in John is pretty long, and there are a number of really good themes we could focus on], but this morning I'd like us to consider what Jesus was saying, "God is spirit, and those who worship Him must worship him in spirit and in truth."   In spirit and in truth.

I believe this scripture has something important to tell us about worship, about how we should be worshiping.

Jesus pointed to our spiritual lives when he told the woman about the Living Water that he would give her. The Living Water was not for her physical needs, but it would become as a spring of water gushing up for eternal life. How precious that would be--to have access to a spiritual spring of water that is continuously gushing, providing much needed refreshment to our spirits!

How quickly our spiritual wells can run dry. I've heard Dave speak of people or situations that dry his very bones! What a descriptive picture! What an awful picture! But, we have all known 'bone-parching' times in life, when something good inside us seems to dry up and leave us spiritually thirsty, gasping for refreshment.

Worship is about coming to the LORD for refreshment, solace, and recharging. I think it's a matter of laying down the burdens in life, 'letting go and letting God.' We come to fill our spirits with the Living Water that Jesus provides.

The living water fills our spirits in the same what the fresh, sweet, spring water refreshes our mouths and bodies. It washes out the bad taste and staleness of our dry mouths and makes us feel clean and good inside.

Without his gift of Living Water, we would be in a terrible fix. Jesus said that this Living Water gushes into us forever. There is no end to it. When we tap into the Living Water we have it from now on.

Worship is all about communing with God, coming to God with the troubles of the day, the concerns we are carrying around and leaving them with the LORD. He told us to 'come, all you who are hardworking and heaven laden, and [he] will give you rest.' (Matt 11:28)

God is spirit, and those who worship Him must worship in spirit and in truth.

Before the woman could hear Jesus' offer of Living Water, she had to come to an understanding of the truth about herself.

She knew her own story very well … but she did not realize that Jesus knew it, too.

Her story was not any more or less colorful than our own stories are. She was a woman who had seen a lot of life. Maybe she had buried some of her husbands. Maybe she really was a terrible cook. Maybe she had a terrible tongue. She had hurt some, and she had been hurt by others. She was really an example of each of us.

She stood in the need of Jesus' grace, in need of his Living Water.

The woman could not receive the Living Water that Jesus was ready to give until she came to terms with herself. When Jesus told her to go get her husband, it caused her to look squarely at the person she really was and what she really needed.

That's what this story is telling us. First we have to look at our lives ... the way that God looks at them. We cannot gloss over the pain or the loss or the hurt that we have known. We cannot treat lightly the times we have been the cause of hurt for others.

Before we can taste the Living Waters which will not run dry, we need to see ourselves as God knows us to be. We need to know our own stories:

- Know when we felt lost or alone
- When did we know we believed in Christ?
- When did we have a mountain top experience?
- When did we fail miserably?
- When did we ask for forgiveness?
- When did we accept forgiveness?
- When did we forgive ourselves?
- When did we find ourselves walking with the LORD?
- When did we share Christ with others?

Jesus knows our stories. Jesus knows the whole of our stories, even the parts we don't want to remember; even the parts we can't forget or forgive. Jesus is all about making us whole people—filled with his spirit and following him.

When we come to Jesus we bring our whole selves along. If we bring only our physical bodies, our minds and hearts can be wandering all over the place, and we're not worshiping.

Jesus tells us when we come to worship, we must worship in spirit and in truth.

After Jesus and the woman at the well had finished their conversations, the disciples returned with lunch. St. John tells us that the woman left the well and ran back to town. I can just imagine her being so excited about meeting Jesus, the man who told her all about herself and who invited her into relationship with the Living God, that she nearly skipped or ran all the way back into town. And when she got there she couldn't help but shout from the top of her voice what she had heard and seen. She had seen the Messiah! She had met a man who knew all about who she was, who had told her everything there was to be known about her. She was full of the spirit! Sounds like those disciples on the day of Pentecost.

In this scripture Jesus is telling us something we need to hear: worshiping God is done 'in spirit and in truth.'

It occurs to me that worship is not a spectator sport, although I'm sure there are some good arguments to the contrary. But Jesus' own words are telling us something different. Jesus said true worshipers will worship in spirit and in truth.

We need to prepare our hearts for worship when we come together. If we don't prepare ourselves we may wonder, 'what happened to me today? Did I find something important to my faith-walk with Jesus today? Was there any real difference between coming to God's house today and staying at home and reading the newspaper?'

When we're not prepared for worship, we are most likely operating from our physical self. We may be thinking:

- About our comfort in the pews
- What songs we enjoy singing and hearing or what we wish we heard
- Music that we don't like; and why are we singing that today?
- Whether we agree with the way the service has been laid out
- Are we happy with the way the service flows?
- Letting our minds wander to many secular concerns

We need to come to worship recognizing that our spiritual water buckets need filling,

- preparing ourselves for worship

- Remembering 'a broken and a contrite heart [God] will not despise'
- Come knowing that we need the gift of Living Water
- We need to be expectant that something good, something wonderful will happen in
- our hearts today.
- We need to be listening to the words in scripture, prayer and song
- Listening for God's voice speaking to us
- It may be a smile of a friend that encourages us
- Or maybe we have an opportunity to bring some joy in someone else's life.
- We need to be ready to be filled with the spring of water that will never run dry.
- Looking forward to being made new, once again, with Jesus' wonderful spirit.

John 6: 1-15

6 Some time after this, Jesus crossed to the far shore of the Sea of Galilee (that is, the Sea of Tiberias), 2 and a great crowd of people followed him because they saw the signs he had performed by healing the sick. 3 Then Jesus went up on a mountainside and sat down with his disciples. 4 The Jewish Passover Festival was near.

5 When Jesus looked up and saw a great crowd coming toward him, he said to Philip, "Where shall we buy bread for these people to eat?" 6 He asked this only to test him, for he already had in mind what he was going to do.

7 Philip answered him, "It would take more than half a year's wages[a] to buy enough bread for each one to have a bite!"

8 Another of his disciples, Andrew, Simon Peter's brother, spoke up,9 "Here is a boy with five small barley loaves and two small fish, but how far will they go among so many?"

10 Jesus said, "Have the people sit down." There was plenty of grass in that place, and they sat down (about five thousand men were there).11 Jesus then took the loaves, gave thanks, and distributed to those who were seated as much as they wanted. He did the same with the fish.

¹² When they had all had enough to eat, he said to his disciples, "Gather the pieces that are left over. Let nothing be wasted." ¹³ So they gathered them and filled twelve baskets with the pieces of the five barley loaves left over by those who had eaten.

¹⁴ After the people saw the sign Jesus performed, they began to say, "Surely this is the Prophet who is to come into the world." ¹⁵ Jesus, knowing that they intended to come and make him king by force, withdrew again to a mountain by himself.

A MESSAGE AS BIG AS LIFE

Today's theme is about messages. Don't we love to get messages?

These days we have new ways of receiving messages. We have email, which helps many of us communicate quickly and across wide stretches with very little cost. Email is very handy. We have lots of ways we communicate electronically. There's telephone, radio, T.V., cell phones, short wave, and probably lots of ways I don't even know. But sometimes it's very nice to receive a hand written note from someone. Someone took the time to write out a message and stamp it and take it to the mailbox.

Messages are important because they help us communicate. They help us hear from someone who is not nearby.

I wonder if we can say what Jesus' message was? We ought to know … We're Christians, the ones who are witnesses of Christ. But what can we actually say about his message? Can it be bottled up in one phrase or word?

I suppose we might say Jesus' message was love. Love God and love one another. Love our neighbor as ourselves. That's good. Certainly, Jesus' message was about love.

Maybe we could say it was about the Kingdom of heaven, the Kingdom of God. We remember Jesus saying many times that the Kingdom of God is at hand or coming soon ... That someone was not far from the Kingdom of God. Jesus told many parables about the Kingdom of God—the Kingdom of God is like the tiniest seed of all that grows into the greatest plant of all; the Kingdom of God is like a man who finds a treasure buried in a field and he goes and sells all and buys the field; the Kingdom of God is like a woman who has lost a coin and she sweeps her house carefully until she finds the coin and then she calls the village to rejoice with her that she has found the coin. There must be hundreds of sayings about the Kingdom.

How about discipleship? Jesus talked much about discipleship, how to go the extra mile, how to give a cloak as well as a shirt; how to turn the other cheek; how to give generously and not just from our spare change. Jesus had so many wise sayings—you are the salt of the earth; you are the light of the world. Let your light shine for the world to see.

Maybe that is what Jesus' message was about.

Maybe we can find Jesus' message every time we hear a story about Jesus. Maybe we can discover Jesus' message in our lesson today.

This lesson is really special. We find it in St. John, chapter 6. We can also find this same story in all four Gospels. In fact it is the only miracle story of Jesus that is found in all four gospels.

It starts out with Jesus being surrounded by the crowds of people. You have to understand that Jesus was very, very popular with people, everyday people. When he came into the neighborhood, people must have stopped what they were doing to go listen to him. It must have become almost like a national holiday when Jesus came to town.

Word spread quickly about Jesus coming and people began to follow him, wherever he went.

Jesus had been teaching and preaching and healing people for some time when this story began, so Jesus decided to take his inner circle of followers and move away from the crowds. They jumped in a boat on the Sea of Galilee and sailed across to another little town about 4 miles away. The people saw where the boat was heading and decided to take the land path to the little town.

It wasn't long after Jesus and his disciples had landed in the new area and begun to move up the hill that the saw the mass of people arriving to hear more from Jesus.

At this point we have to imagine this scene. The people were flooding up the hill and drawing near to Jesus. They must have been pretty tired because they had just walked about nine miles to get to the same place the boat had taken four miles to attain.

Jesus looked out on the people and had compassion on them. He realized that they needed refreshment.

Jesus looked at Philip and asked him, "Where can we find food for all these people?" Jesus asked Philip because he was from this village and he would know what was available there.

But Philip was astounded at his Lord's question. Surely Jesus would know that feeding all these people even a little would be an enormous task, one that would take over 6 months' wages. He said this to Jesus.

Then Andrew, Simon Peter's brother, came up to Jesus with a young boy with him. Andrew told Jesus that this child had some food with him—5 loaves and 2 fish—but what could that do among so many people?

Jesus told the disciples to have the people sit down on the ground. He then took the loaves and blessed them and gave them to the people. He then did the same with the fish, giving them out to the people.

The people ate and were filled! It was a miracle! Everyone was satisfied. Each person ate as much as he or she wanted.

The crowd numbered five thousand men not including women and children. So we know there were many more than just 5 thousand.

This story in John is a wonderful story of Jesus doing a miracle, providing a meal for so many people, and it has an echo in the Hebrew Bible.

Think back to the time when the Israelites were wandering in the desert after they had been freed of their slavery in Egypt. Moses had led them to freedom and there they were in the desert, maybe a million people, wandering and wondering where they were going to find water or food. They weren't able to carry enough with them from Egypt for the rest of their lives.

They were in a scary place then. They were lost and hungry; their children didn't have any food and neither did anyone else. They complained to their leader, Moses, and said they would just as soon be slaves in Egypt as die of starvation in the desert.

Moses went to the Lord in prayer and asked for help. Moses went to the one who had sent him on his mission to begin with--the one he had met in the burning bush. The one who had called himself the "I AM who I AM." The great EXISTENT ONE.

And God sent food to the people. I hope you remember the story; God sent manna from heaven every morning. The manna appeared on the ground like dew on the grass. It was maybe like frosted flakes all over the ground. The manna was tasty and nourishing. It was gathered by everyone each morning and provided them a break to their fast each day. The 'manna' mean, "What is it?" What is it? It was what God had provided for the wanderers. The manna kept coming every morning for 40 years, all the time they lived in the wilderness.

God provided for the hungry people. Jesus provided for the mass of people who were hungry.

Jesus tells us that he never did anything but what God did. He saw what God was doing on the earth and he did the same—healing, feeding, teaching, guiding, loving.

Jesus did many wonderful miracles; told many wonderful parables, spoke wonderful words of wisdom and help. He challenged people to come to him and trust in him. Jesus called people to follow him.

There are many religions in this world, way more than I know much about. But Christianity stands by itself. Our faith is the only religion that is based on a person. Every other religion is based on ideas—philosophy. Some religions tell us to think this way or that. Some religions say we should deny our passions. Some religions say we should try to be moderate in all things. Some religions say we should follow many, many rules. All those religions are about ideas, things you can't touch.

Christianity is based on one person, Jesus of Nazareth. Jesus is the message. His coming to earth was part of God's wonderful plan from the beginning. Jesus' message is himself.

Yesterday I was thinking about the message and the messenger. We've heard that expression, the messenger was killed when he gave the message. I don't think that saying came from Christ, because, a thousand years before that, King David heard from a messenger about King Saul's death, and he had the messenger killed! The saying is don't shoot the messenger; he's only the messenger.

But in Jesus' case he was the messenger and he was the message. And they killed him. His message was love from God to us. His death shows us how much God is willing to give in order to communicate his love to us.

Jesus is the messenger and the message, a message as big as life.

He shows us in every way how much he loves us by how much he gave us. When Jesus fed the thousands, he was reminding us of his love and care and passion for us.

We are called to be like Christ. If we've accepted the gift of life and salvation through our faith in Christ, we need to be about growing more and more like him.

What is our message today? Yes, Jesus is the message sent from God, and we share in his love and in blessing one another.

John 6: 66-69 NRSV

66 Because of this many of his disciples turned back and no longer went about with him. 67 So Jesus asked the twelve, "Do you also wish to go away?" 68 Simon Peter answered him, "Lord, to whom can we go? You have the words of eternal life. 69 We have come to believe and know that you are the Holy One of God."[a]

IF YOU HEAR GOD'S VOICE

I'd like to tell you about Miss Alice. I knew her when we lived in Wiesbaden, Germany, when our big kids were small. I took piano lessons from Miss Alice. She was our chapel choir pianist, and she was a very good musician.

One day when I went for my lesson she told me that she was expecting a very important phone call. The phone call was from a friend she knew from childhood when she lived in Latvia. Miss Alice and her childhood friend were very good friends, but during the War they were both taken to different work camps by the Nazis. They never saw one another again, because after the war Miss Alice came to Germany, but her friend was sent by the Russians to the most northern town in Siberia.

Somehow they kept in touch. They began writing letters back and forth. Their lives were very different, but they could communicate.

Miss Alice told me that her friend had told her phone lines had finally been put in her town and that she could call Miss Alice the following week.

When I arrived at my lesson, Miss Alice had just hung up the phone, having spoken to her good friend. She was elated! She was full of the good memories of her friend, and she told me, 'Even though we are both old women today, and so many years had passed since [they] had seen one another, I knew her voice! She sounded exactly like she did when we were 20 years old!'

There are many voices we hear in our world—voices that come from many places. You might say that voices contain the words which make up our humanity.

What voices do we hear? Voices of our community—family, friends, co-workers, neighbors. I think we all listen to voices of people we love and admire better than we do to voices of people who we consider 'suspect' or foreign. That's just human nature. In fact, because we do listen better to voices close to us, that's what helps us retain our cultural position.

Think of it. We're much more likely to listen to someone we know and trust than to listen to someone from outside our comfort zone, or voices from another world.

Voices from our past—our parents, our schoolmates, long-ago friends. We'll live forever hearing the voices of our parents. I love to be able to pick up the phone and talk with my Mom, but I hear her voice many times from the past—without benefit of the telephone. Mother will always be with me in her voice.

Same thing goes for valued friends. We don't forget their voices.

Our own voice has a greater authority than do many other voices. We may limit ourselves or allow us to achieve things because of how we talk to ourselves. We say things like:

- I've never lost a pound; I can't lose weight.
- I don't know how to run, or swim, or … draw. I can't do that.
- I don't like to read; there's nothing interesting to read.
- I can't do math. I don't like 'story problems'.
- I'm afraid of … what? Spiders? Snakes? Big dogs?

We accomplish good things by being positive in our talking to ourselves. When we go at a project with a positive attitude, saying, 'Self, I can do this. I've managed tough things in the past; I know I can do this, too. Especially with the LORD's help.' We have a much better chance of success with a positive attitude.

Voices are very important to us every day. We live in such a world of voices coming from every direction. They each have influence on us— positive or negative. Some voices we will never listen to because we've had a bad experience with that voice before. Others we always trust, no matter what. That might also be dangerous. We need to find a voice that we can trust no matter what ... a voice that we can judge all other voices by.

In John's gospel we read about Jesus and his many followers. This was during Jesus' ministry, but it wasn't the early part; it was somewhere in the middle of his ministry. Jesus had been talking to his many followers for some time, and some of them were beginning to fall away from following him. There was something that caused them to fall away.

They had experienced many wonderful things with Jesus. They had witnessed Jesus' feeding some 5000 men plus women and children with just a few loaves and a couple of fish. They had seen him heal many people of sickness. They had heard many wonderful parables about the Kingdom of Heaven.

But something had caused many of the followers to fall way. John tells us that they decided that they could not accept something that Jesus had said.

When Jesus saw so many of these followers falling away, shaking their heads and returning home, Jesus turned to his inner group of disciples and asked them, 'Will you leave me too?'

Peter spoke up and said, *'Lord, where can we go? You have the words of eternal life.'*

I think Peter had a moment of enlightenment just then. We know he also answered another time when Jesus asked, *'Who do you say that I am?'* Peter said, *'You are the Christ of God.'* And Jesus told Peter then that he could not have said that on his own, but that he was given that knowledge from the Holy Spirit.

'You have the words of eternal life.' Eternal life comes from God. Peter spoke those words for each of us. When we come to that same conclusion, we must ask his question, too: Where can we go when we realize that Jesus has the words of eternal life?' Is there some compromise we can get by with?

Is there some way to accept some of what Jesus said, but not the hard sayings?

Jesus said some tough things:

- Follow me
- Take up the cross and follow him
- Give all our wealth to the poor and follow him
- Go the second mile
- Give your shirt as well as you coat
- Love your enemies, not just your friends
- Put God first in your life
- Be nourished by Jesus' blood and body.
- Take Jesus into ourselves and abide in him.

Those are hard words, and some followers decided they couldn't accept them. Following Jesus is not easy, but Peter said, 'Where else can we go? There is no other way. Once you've found THE way. Jesus told us, *'I am the Way the Truth and the Life; on one comes to the Father except through Me.'* (John 14:6)

When we follow Jesus we are saying, 'Yes' to Him. "Yes, Lord, I will follow you.'

That's the sinner's prayer. You admit your need for Jesus. You admit that you are a fallen creature; you have sinned and need Jesus' salvation. "Yes, Lord Jesus, I take you as my savior.'

There's a problem with that, though. The problem is that saying, 'Yes' the first time to

Jesus is opening the door to saying, 'Yes' again and again and again. The problem is that down the road we don't know what Jesus will be asking us to say, 'yes' to. What if it's not convenient?

'Where can we go' You, [Jesus], have the words of eternal life.' Those are Peter's words; those are our words, too.

Miss Sarah Corson, who is an Alabama UM missionary, spent much time in Bolivia teaching and sharing Christ. She wrote about a man from Bolivia that came into her town one day.

The man lived in a very remote village high in the Andes Mountains. He had to walk a long, treacherous route to get to her town.

The man's name was Rene'. He had heard on the radio that there was going to be a Christian medical team in the town, so he made the effort to come see them. But Rene didn't need to see a doctor, he just wanted to meet some Christians.

Rene' told Sarah how his little village didn't know about Jesus. They worshiped great stone images that were made by their ancestors. They sacrificed sheep and llamas to these images, even when their children were undernourished.

Rene' said that a man had come to his village the year before to tell his people about Jesus, but he was run out by the people. They wanted to stone hm. Before he left, though, he managed to shove a book into Rene's hands and tell him, 'Read this book, it had the words of God in it.'

Rene' read the book, which was the Bible, and he believed. He recognized the words in the Bible were words from God. He could hear the voice of God in those pages, and he wanted to respond by following Christ.

Jesus said, "I am the bread of life. Your ancestors ate the manna in the wilderness, and they died. This is the bread that comes down from Heaven, so that one may eat of it and not die. I am the living bread that came down from heaven. Whoever eats of this bread will life forever, and the bread that I will give for the life of the world is my flesh.'

9 *As he walked along, he saw a man blind from birth. 2 His disciples asked him, "Rabbi, who sinned, this man or his parents, that he was born blind?" 3 Jesus answered, "Neither this man nor his parents sinned; he was born blind so that God's works might be revealed in him. 4 We[a] must work the works of him who sent me[b] while it is day; night is coming when no one can work. 5 As long as I am in the world, I am the light of the world." 6 When he had said this, he spat on the ground and made mud with the saliva and spread the mud on the man's eyes, 7 saying to him, "Go, wash in the pool of Siloam" (which means Sent). Then he went and washed and came back able to see. 8 The neighbors and those who had seen him before as a beggar began to ask, "Is this* not the man who used to sit and beg?" 9 Some were saying, "It is he." Others were saying, "No, but it is someone like him." He kept saying, "I am the man." 10 But they kept asking him, "Then how were your eyes opened?" 11 He answered, "The man called Jesus made mud, spread it on my eyes, and said to me, 'Go to Siloam and wash.' Then I went and washed and received my sight." 12 They said to him, "Where is he?" He said, "I do not know."

13 They brought to the Pharisees the man who had formerly been blind.14 Now it was a sabbath day when Jesus made the mud and opened his eyes. 15 Then the Pharisees also began to ask him how he had received his sight. He said to them, "He put mud on my eyes. Then I washed, and now I see." 16 Some of the Pharisees said, "This man is not from God, for he

does not observe the sabbath." But others said, "How can a man who is a sinner perform such signs?" And they were divided. ₁₇ So they said again to the blind man, "What do you say about him? It was your eyes he opened." He said, "He is a prophet."

₁₈ The Jews did not believe that he had been blind and had received his sight until they called the parents of the man who had received his sight₁₉ and asked them, "Is this your son, who you say was born blind? How then does he now see?" ₂₀ His parents answered, "We know that this is our son, and that he was born blind; ₂₁ but we do not know how it is that now he sees, nor do we know who opened his eyes. Ask him; he is of age. He will speak for himself." ₂₂ His parents said this because they were afraid of the Jews; for the Jews had already agreed that anyone who confessed Jesus[c] to be the Messiah[d] would be put out of the synagogue. 23 Therefore his parents said, "He is of age; ask him."

24 So for the second time they called the man who had been blind, and they said to him, "Give glory to God! We know that this man is a sinner."25 He answered, "I do not know whether he is a sinner. One thing I do know, that though I was blind, now I see." 26 They said to him, "What did he do to you? How did he open your eyes?" 27 He answered them, "I have told you already, and you would not listen. Why do you want to hear it again? Do you also want to become his disciples?" 28 Then they reviled him, saying, "You are his disciple, but we are disciples of Moses.29 We know that God has spoken to Moses, but as for this man, we do

not know where he comes from." 30 The man answered, "Here is an astonishing thing! You do not know where he comes from, and yet he opened my eyes. 31 We know that God does not listen to sinners, but he does listen to one who worships him and obeys his will. 32 Never since the world began has it been heard that anyone opened the eyes of a person born blind. 33 If this man were not from God, he could do nothing." 34 They answered him, "You were born entirely in sins, and are you trying to teach us?" And they drove him out.

35 Jesus heard that they had driven him out, and when he found him, he said, "Do you believe in the Son of Man?"[c] 36 He answered, "And who is he, sir?[i] Tell me, so that I may believe in him." 37 Jesus said to him, "You have seen him, and the

one speaking with you is he." 38 He said, "Lord,[a] I believe." And he worshiped him. 39 Jesus said, "I came into this world for judgment so that those who do not see may see, and those who do see may become blind." 40 Some of the Pharisees near him heard this and said to him, "Surely we are not blind, are we?" 41 Jesus said to them, "If you were blind, you would not have sin. But now that you say, 'We see,' your sin remains.

SEEING IS BELIEVING

John tells us another story in Chapter Nine. Jesus heals a blind man. Jesus healed a man, not just blind, but a man who had been blind from birth. He was seriously blind.

We don't know about being blind. We live in a world that is much dependent on good sight. Some of us have less than 20-20 vision these days, but most of us have a correctable vision with glasses or laser surgery. We are very dependent on our sight, and we are pretty happy with it.

I have a friend, Mr. Bob Sloan, who has some disease of the eye, which is genetic. (His mother also had the same trouble.) His vision has gone from good to a pinhole view of the world. Because of his vision trouble, he can't drive a car or do a lot of things we just take for granted. Bob gets along quite well; he has a full, good life, but his vision isn't good.

I imagine many of us have been in a totally black place before, maybe in a cavern where no light can come in. You go into the cavern with some kind of flashlight or even overhead lights of a kind, and then the guide turns off the lights, and PITCH BLACK! It's eerie! You could very quickly lose your bearings in pitch black.

The other night, as we were making our way to the bedroom, closing down the house, locking the doors, snapping off the lights, I had arrived in the bedroom first. A couple of minutes later I heard a strange sound and then a thud! What was that? I went to the living room to see Dave was picking himself up off the floor. He had come into the living room, which I had made dark by snapping off the light. He tripped over Snoopy, which caused him to fall into a glass table in the living room! The glass table has a metal sculpture on it, and Dave fell into that, which caused the tail of the whale sculpture to dig into his hand and fly across the room!

Gads! Dave was damaged; the glass table was almost damaged. We were glad more damage had not occurred because of the fall. I have vowed not to be so careful about reducing the lights in the house. The last person through the house should be the one to turn off the lights.

Light in this world plays an important roll. My cousin, Steve Pile, lives in northern Alaska. He's a teaching-principal at a school for native American children. Where he lives the sun does a really strange thing. It sinks lower and lower in the horizon each day beginning with fall, until it is totally gone for several months! The people have to learn to function daily just the way we would if it was always midnight. How very strange! How very disorienting!

Light is a real part of our lives, and we take it for granted most of the time. We not only enjoy having light in our world and realize the importance of having light, light is also a great metaphor.

We say, 'let's shine a bit more light on the subject', meaning we'd like to see/understand something better. We need more information about the subject.

We say, 'don't hide your light under a bushel', which is, of course, a direct quote from Jesus. Jesus said, [14]*"You are the light of the world. A city built on a hill cannot be hid. [15]No one after lighting a lamp puts it under the bushel basket, but on the lampstand, and it gives light to all in the house. [16]In the same way, let your light shine before others, so that they may see your good works and give glory to your Father in heaven*

We need light in our lives to navigate in this world. It is not impossible to live in the world without light, but light is very helpful. Without light we must rely on many other ways to negotiate our way around.

So light has become a wonderful picture, a metaphor, for the need we have as spiritual people, as we try to navigate our way through life. We need spiritual light. We are in the dark without spiritual light.

John's story of Jesus healing the man blind from birth needs to be viewed from two levels. Most scriptures in Bible have both a literal and a spiritual message for us. I think it's always a good idea to begin with the literal meaning of the passage, understand it from that perspective, and then work on how the scripture can also have a spiritual message for us.

In this scripture Jesus healed the man born blind; he gave him his sight.

That had to be a remarkable moment in the man's life. His world changed forever the day that Jesus gave him his sight. Suddenly the man had a new way of understanding the world. It would have taken some time for the man to learn to interpret the messages his eyes were sending his brain, so he would know what he was looking at. If you have never seen a chair or a house or a donkey before, it might take time to make sense out of the message your brain is sending you.

The man had a whole new set of opportunities in life, now that he had sight. He could learn to read and write. His life was no longer limited to begging for a living. He could learn to farm or be a shepherd or fish or… or … or … whatever he chose.

The message from Scripture would be very good, if it only had the message that Jesus healed the man born blind. It would be another wonderful example of the healing that Jesus does, daily, for us. But there is more.

The story definitely has a second meaning, a spiritual meaning.

The Jews were upset about the newly-sighted man. They questioned him and then his parents, to be sure they had the facts of his healing. They asked, "Are you sure this is your son? Are you sure he was born blind, not able to see at all?"

The newly sighted man, finally says, *'One thing I do know, that though I was blind, now I see.'* He didn't know who it was who had healed him. Jesus had come to the man, made a paste of mud and applied it to the man's eyes, and then Jesus told the man to go to the Pool of Siloam and wash. So when the man began to see, Jesus was not in sight.

But the man understood more than the Jews did. He realized that he had been touched by the hand of God, when he was healed. The Jews were hollering that they didn't know where Jesus came from, or if he had any credentials that would give him the power to heal someone. They said, 'We know that God has spoken to Moses, but as for this man, we do not know where he comes from.'

We can imagine what it's like to be physically blind, and we know we would not like it. Physical blindness would alter our lives in a significant way. We would find all our relationships changing and our possibilities in this life, too.

But we don't much think about what spiritual blindness would mean to us. Might we not have perfect vision, spiritually? Of course, there's no test, like you find at the eye doctor's office that could assess our spiritual visioning. But we can tell something about a person's spiritual vision by the way they lead their lives.

Jesus, using a different metaphor, says we can know a tree by the fruit it produces. So perhaps, we can understand something about our spiritual vision acuity by the fruit we produce.

We might ask about our life:

> Is it glorifying to God?

> Is it humble?

> Does it love beyond the close family and friends?

We've been thinking about how Jesus healed the man born blind, but he wasn't completelyblind. His blindness was limited to his eyes. His spiritual acuity was working fine. Listen to what the newly sighted man said to the Pharisees: *'Here is an astonishing thing! You do not know where [this man, Jesus,] comes from, and yet he opened my eyes. We know that God does not listen to sinners, but he does listen to one who worships and obeys his will. Never since the world began has it been heard that anyone opened the eyes of a person born blind. If this man were not from God, he could do nothing."*

The newly-sighted man may have been blind his whole life, but he spiritual vision wasn't too bad. He could see what the Pharisees didn't see.

The very last words in Chapter Nine come from Jesus, speaking to the Pharisees.

35Jesus heard that they had driven him out, and when he found him, he said, "Do you believe in the Son of Man?" 36He answered, "And who is he, sir? Tell me, so that I may believe in him." 37Jesus said to him, "You have seen him, and the one speaking with you is he." 38He said, "Lord, I believe." And he worshiped him. 39Jesus said, "I came into this world for judgment so that those who do not see may see, and those who do see may become blind." 40Some of the Pharisees near him heard this and said to him, "Surely we are not blind, are we?" 41 Jesus said to them, "If you were blind, you would not have sin. But now that you say, 'We see,' your sin remains.

The man didn't immediately recognize Jesus, because he had not seen him when his sight was given him, but the minute Jesus told him about his healing, the man responded by telling of his faith in Jesus and worshiping him.

On the other hand, there are the Pharisees. They were the people that were supposed to have spiritual insight. Yet they scoffed at Jesus' healing the blind man, because he was healed on the Sabbath, and they suggested that Jesus was in league with the devil. Their spiritual eyes were seriously out of focus.

Jesus said, *"I came into this world for judgment so that those who do not see may see, and those who do see may become blind."*

To this the Pharisees objected, and hollered back, 'surely we are not blind!"

41 Jesus said to them, "If you were blind, you would not have sin. But now that you say, 'We see,' your sin remains.

Jesus is telling us that there is a difference between those who are using their spiritual vision and those who do not.

When we are using our spiritual vision we will see that Jesus was doing God's will and acting for God on this earth. "No one ever has given sight to someone blind from birth.

There's a double standard here. Do you see it?

I think my spiritual eyes have been opened some this week, as I've wrestled with this pericope. Jesus is telling us that there are some people who don't have the same opportunities for seeing him on this earth.

We are judged according to the light that we have.

Jesus said a mouthful just then. First, *'If you were blind, you would not have sin.'* Jesus is not meaning physical blindness, but being 'spiritually blind'. The Pharisees, who were normally sighted, could not see with spiritual eyes the things that Jesus was doing came from God. (Nobody had ever given sight to someone born blind before.) They said he was in league with the devil. That's being very short-sighted, spiritually.

His words angered the Pharisees, and they drove him out of the Temple.

At six weeks of age Miss Frances Jane Crosby was given eye suave that caused her to become permanently blind! Fanny lived the rest of her life without any sight. Fanny Crosby may have spent the rest of her near-century of life not being able to see the world, but in a more important way Fanny was not blind at all. Her spiritual sightedness was clearer than it is for many of us. Her faith in the risen LORD gave her words that she shared with the world.

She knew Jesus, her Lord, and she followed him. She knew his voice, and she was sure of his guiding her. Fanny was not blind where it really counts. Her physical blindness might have even aided her spiritual vision.

Hear in her own words

All the way my Savior leads me
What have I to ask beside
Can I doubt His faithful mercies
Who through life has been my guide
Heavenly peace, divinest comfort
ere by faith in Him to dwell
for I know whatever fall me
Jesus doeth all things well

All of the way my Savior leads me
and He cheers each winding path I tread
gives me strength for every trial
and He feeds me with the living bread
and though my weary steps may falter
and my soul a thirst may be
gushing from a rock before me
though a spirit joy I see

And all the way my Savior leads me
oh the fullness of His love
perfect rest in me is promised
in my Father's house above
when my spirit clothed immortal
wings its flight to realms of day
this my song through endless ages
Jesus led me all the way

John 10:10 NRSV

[10] *The thief comes only to steal and kill and destroy. I came that they may have life, and have it abundantly.*

THAT'S LIVING!

Long before Terry Shaivo was heard about on T.V., she was suffering from a terrible problem. She had an eating disorder which caused her to bilge (eat way too much) and then purge the food, throwing it up. By doing this again and again and again, Terry had caused her body to lose too much phosphorus, which caused her to have a serious stroke, leaving her in that terrible state of partial consciousness. That's not living!

I suppose there are many people in this world like Bob. As a young man, Bob was a very handsome man. He was even a male model in one of the national clothing catalogs—I think it was for Penney's. Bob cut a wonderful figure. He was also very successful in business. He sold Dictaphones and had a good slice of the market in Denver in the fifties. But gradually his business lost out, maybe due to new technology. Bob suffered severe financial reverses and found himself deeply in debt. He lost his house. Other factors must have been at work in Bob's life, because he was turning into a sour old man. His language became vile. He put down his wife whenever he could. Bob's eyesight dimmed, so he could no longer drive.

Today Bob has become a very bitter old man. That's not living.

For some people memories are painful. Even if painful memories have been suppressed from consciousness, pain from the past can continue to affect us today. Some people act out or have difficulties with relationship now, because of pain from their past. That's not living.

There are some people who have suffered disappointment in life and are not happy campers now. They put all their eggs in the one basket, so to speak, and when the basket dropped and the eggs crushed, leaving them lost and alone, they don't know where to go from there. That's not living.

When a person is caught up in the 'what ifs' or the 'if only', blaming themselves or circumstances for changes in their lives that they can't cope with, that's not living.

There are some people who have lost a loved one to death or heartbreak and they can't move on. They are stuck in the cycle of pain and grief over the loss. Their lives seem to have stopped at the moment of loss. They may be alive, but really, that's not living.

We're here today because Jesus came to bring us life and to give it to us abundantly. That's what he told us in John: *I came that they may have life and hate it abundantly.*

I hope you heard those words carefully. Jesus wasn't speaking about everyone in this case, but to a specific group. He was talking about the sheep in his flock. The ones that call him the Good Shepherd.

The Good Shepherd cares for his sheep, which is not what the way of the hired hand or the thief in the night. They have no real interest in the sheep other than to do what they want to do—to rob and kill the sheep.

According to this Scripture there are five qualities that make up the sheep in this flock.

They hear Jesus' voice.

They follow Jesus.

They don't listen to the voices in this world that would lead them astray.

They will be saved

They will come in and go out and find pasture.

It is these sheep about whom Jesus says, "I have come to give life and give it abundantly.

This morning I would like to look at these qualities to understand better what it is to have abundant life.

First the sheep hears his voice.

The sheep have learned to recognize the voice of the Good Shepherd. They have distinguished it from all the other voices in the world and know when they hear when he is calling them.

I wonder if you can say that you know when you hear Jesus' voice speaking to you? I have a feeling that Jesus speaks to us more often than we know, but we're pretty good a shutting out his voice. We don't want to hear it often.

We are comforted when we hear the voice of our Shepherd.

> His voice is encouraging.

> He brings calm to our day.

> His voice instills confident in us.

> His voice tells us he cares for us.

> His voice tells us we belong to him

We know his voice even when it is still and small and heard through the din of the other voices clamoring in the day.

The Sheep of the flock know Jesus' voice.

Jesus told a story we find in Matthew chapter 25, which is also about sheep and goats.

Seems this is about Judgment Day, when Jesus will come to judge all the nations, and he will separate them out the same way a shepherd divides the sheep from the goats. The sheep will be at his right hand and will come into enjoy the pleasures of the Kingdom, but the goats will be sent to his left hand where there will be weeping and gnashing of teeth. Nobody wants to be judged a goat.

Seems the difference between sheep and goats is their ability to hear their master's voice. And the sheep didn't even quite realize that's what they were doing. Jesus said that the sheep had heard the voice of those who were hungry or thirsty or alone and they responded by feeding and giving drink and visiting them. The sheep saw those who were naked and clothed them. They visited them in prison. They had done those things because they had heard their master's voice, and they were led into the Kingdom. What's interesting is that the goats cried out and asked the shepherd, "When did you cry and show need? We would have been right there for you, if only we had known that you were in need. The Good Shepherd told them that since they had not cared for those who were hungry or thirsty or naked or alone, they had not heard his voice.

The sheep of the Good Shepherd's flock follow Jesus. They not only hear his voice, but they follow him. They don't turn back. They keep refocusing their feet on the pathway and they follow him.

They follow him because he knows where the eating is good.

They follow him because he knows where danger lurks.

They follow him because he has told them to be obedient, and they are learning to follow.

They follow him because he is the greatest leader of all.

They follow him because he cares for them.

They follow him because he gives them what they need.

They follow him because he helps them to grow.

They follow him because he forgives them.

The sheep of the Good Shepherd's flock don't listen to the voices of others who want to confuse them and lead them astray.

They don't listen to the alluring voices of get rich quick schemes. The don't listen to voices that tell them that they have to have the newest, most expensive thing. They don't listen to voices that tell them to overspend on their credit cards. They don't listen to voices that tell them they always need new stuff—new cars, new clothes, new stuff.

The sheep of the Good Shepherd's flock will be saved!!!!!

They know that the Good Shepherd has already laid down his life for them. They have nothing to fear. The Good Shepherd has already done everything necessary for them to be saved.

Their sins will be forgiven.

They have no need for guilt.

They will be saved.

The sheep of the Good Shepherd's flock will come in and go out to find pasture.

They don't have to wait until the end of the age to begin to be free.

They have it now.

They will grow and mature and become the finest sheep that they were meant to be.

The have the freedom to grow.

They have the freedom to explore talents and interests that they might not have dared to tackle before.

They won't have any guilt or fear that would hold them back from becoming the best people that the Good Shepherd had designed them to be.

The will have the freedom to be all that they can be.

They have abundant lives because they are free of fear, free of worry, free of guilt.

They have abundant lives because Jesus, the Good Shepherd, keeps filling them every day with his love. They have abundant lives because Jesus gives them everything they need. They have abundant lives because they will be among the other sheep of the fold who are also being filled with the Shepherd's Spirit.

They have abundant lives because they are enriched by the love from the Savior and from the other sheep.

They have abundant lives because even when difficulties arise, even when there are scary times, even when there is turmoil or confusion, they have the Good Shepherd to guide them and fill them.

They have the confidence of the children of Heaven that everything will all turn out well in the end.

Several years ago I was responsible for the program for the Ladies' Fellowship at the church I was serving, and I invented a game which I thought would be fun, The idea of the game was for each lady to think about various other women in their lives who had done something special for them—taught them to sew or cook or pray; raised them; a special friend…etc. One of the questions was, "Who would you most like to be like? What woman is your ideal?" When I came to put my own answers to that list, I found I couldn't really think of any other woman I would most like to be about. (I do remember one of the ladies said she'd most like to be like Martha Stewart; I wonder if that still holds?) Anyway, after thinking for quite a while, I decided that I really don't want to be like any other woman, I really want to be the woman that our Lord has planned for me to be. That's who I need to be like. Jesus came to give us abundant life.

At about that same time I came to know a family in that community that was having some real trouble. The husband and wife had twin baby daughters, really cute little girls with big blue eyes and blond hair. The trouble was that they were being watched quite carefully by the DHR, the Department of Human Resources, to be sure that those girls were being taken care of properly. The DHR had even contacted the couple's neighbors to instruct them that if there was any indication of inappropriate goings on at their home they must call DHR immediately. The couple suddenly felt like they were living in a fish bowl, with the whole world spying on them all the time. Then one night they were turned in by their neighbors for arguing loudly in the presence of their little girls DHR came and took the children and put them in foster care. The couple were devastated. That's not living!

When I heard about that I mentioned it to my son, Stephen, who was away in BHM at school. He called me the next day and told me that he had just returned from a weekend youth retreat in another city. He and several friends from BSC had been asked to come to do a lock in with a whole bunch of youth and then to help the kids lead in worship on Sunday. After the weekend Stephen and his friends were each paid $100 for their work. When Stephen told one of the other youth workers about the plight of the twin girls, the two of them decided to give their newly earned pay to the girls in the form of a scholarship which would be put aside for them to claim later for college.

Those two young people are members of the flock owned by the Good Shepherd. They heard the voice of their lord in the cries of the twin girls and their parents and responded. I would say, "That's living!

11 *Now a certain man was ill, Lazarus of Bethany, the village of Mary and her sister Martha.* ² *Mary was the one who anointed the Lord with perfume and wiped his feet with her hair; her brother Lazarus was ill.* ³ *So the sisters sent a message to Jesus,[a] "Lord, he whom you love is ill."* ⁴ *But when Jesus heard it, he said, "This illness does not lead to death; rather it is for God's glory, so that the Son of God may be glorified through it."* ⁵ *Accordingly, though Jesus loved Martha and her sister and Lazarus,* ⁶ *after having heard that Lazarus[a] was ill, he stayed two days longer in the place where he was.*

⁷ *Then after this he said to the disciples, "Let us go to Judea again."* ⁸ *The disciples said to him, "Rabbi, the Jews were just now trying to stone you, and are you going there again?"* ⁹ *Jesus answered, "Are there not twelve hours of daylight? Those who walk during the day do not stumble, because they see the light of this world.* ¹⁰ *But those who walk at night stumble, because the light is not in*

them." [11] After saying this, he told them, "Our friend Lazarus has fallen asleep, but I am going there to awaken him." [12] The disciples said to him, "Lord, if he has fallen asleep, he will be all right." [13] Jesus, however, had been speaking about his death, but they thought that he was referring merely to sleep. [14] Then Jesus told them plainly, "Lazarus is dead. [15] For your sake I am glad I was not there, so that you may believe. But let us go to him." [16] Thomas, who was called the Twin,[a] said to his fellow disciples, "Let us also go, that we may die with him."

[17] When Jesus arrived, he found that Lazarus[a] had already been in the tomb four days. [18] Now Bethany was near Jerusalem, some two miles[a] away, [19] and many of the Jews had come to Martha and Mary to console them about their brother. [20] When Martha heard that Jesus was coming, she went and met him, while Mary stayed at home. [21] Martha said to Jesus, "Lord, if you had been here, my brother would not have died. [22] But even now I know that God will give you whatever you ask

of him."²³ Jesus said to her, "Your brother will rise again." ²⁴ Martha said to him, "I know that he will rise again in the resurrection on the last day."²⁵ Jesus said to her, "I am the resurrection and the life.[f] Those who believe in me, even though they die, will live, ²⁶ and everyone who lives and believes in me will never die. Do you believe this?" ²⁷ She said to him, "Yes, Lord, I believe that you are the Messiah,[g] the Son of God, the one coming into the world."

²⁸ When she had said this, she went back and called her sister Mary, and told her privately, "The Teacher is here and is calling for you." ²⁹ And when she heard it, she got up quickly and went to him. ³⁰ Now Jesus had not yet come to the village, but was still at the place where Martha had met him. ³¹ The Jews who were with her in the house, consoling her, saw Mary get up quickly and go out. They followed her because they thought that she was going to the tomb to weep there. ³² When Mary came where Jesus was and saw him, she knelt at his feet and said to him, "Lord, if you had been here, my brother would not have died." ³³ When Jesus saw her weeping, and the Jews who came with her also

weeping, he was greatly disturbed in spirit and deeply moved. 34 He said, "Where have you laid him?" They said to him, "Lord, come and see." 35 Jesus began to weep. 36 So the Jews said, "See how he loved him!" 37 But some of them said, "Could not he who opened the eyes of the blind man have kept this man from dying?"

38 Then Jesus, again greatly disturbed, came to the tomb. It was a cave, and a stone was lying against it. 39 Jesus said, "Take away the stone." Martha, the sister of the dead man, said to him, "Lord, already there is a stench because he has been dead four days." 40 Jesus said to her, "Did I not tell you that if you believed, you would see the glory of God?" 41 So they took away the stone. And Jesus looked upward and said, "Father, I thank you for having heard me. 42 I knew that you always hear me, but I have said this for the sake of the crowd standing here, so that they may believe that you sent me." 43 When he had said this, he cried with a loud voice, "Lazarus, come out!" 44 The dead man came out, his hands and feet bound with strips of cloth, and his face wrapped in a cloth. Jesus said to them, "Unbind him, and let him go."

PRACTICING HIS PRESENCE

It might be interesting to start with a little exercise. Perhaps you've seen it before. I've put little note pages in each bulletin for us, so I would like each of you to spend a minute itemizing the five most important values that you have. Just write them down on your paper. You can list them in order of importance to you, if you would like.

Now, there is a second part to this exercise. I would like each of you to turn your paper over and make a second list. This time I want you to list the five things that fill your day the most.

I suspect that your two lists are not identical. In fact, they may have very little in common.

But that is the way we seem to live our lives. We spend our time on one plane, all the while reserving a second plane for the serious and important, our really big values.

That's what was happening with Martha from Bethany. We remember her from before. She is the older sister of Mary, the woman who sat at Jesus' feet and listened to him teach rather than help Martha with all the responsibilities of hostessin the flock of visitors. This time Martha had a much greater concern. Her brother, Lazarus, had become sick suddenly and had died!

The family lived together, Lazarus, Martha and Mary, in a little town not far from Jerusalem. Today we'd call it a bedroom community of Jerusalem. The town was called Bethany. They were good friends of Jesus. We know from Luke's Gospel that they had a pretty nice place, one that was big and welcomed visitors like Jesus and his disciples. Jesus may have enjoyed spending time with this family on several occasions.

Today's story begins with Jesus and his disciples in a country setting. Outside of Judea. It seems there were some Jewish leaders in Jerusalem that had been so angry with Jesus that they had tried to stone Jesus, so Jesus and his disciples left Jerusalem. They had even left Judea for a safer location.

A message came to Jesus telling him that Lazarus had taken ill. Lazarus' sisters had sent the note. They had not asked Jesus to come to them, but they trusted that Jesus would do the right thing.

Jesus told the disciples about Lazarus being ill, but then he added, *"This illness does not lead to death, rather it is for God's glory, so that the Son of God may be glorified through it."*

Jesus and his disciples remained where they were for two more days, and then Jesus announced that they would return to Bethany. The disciples objected. They were concerned about the danger; they had barely escaped from Judea the last time there were there. It might get nasty if they returned. But Jesus explained that Lazarus had died, then he added, "For your sake I am glad I was not there, so that you may believe. But let us go to him." So they went.

When Jesus arrived near the village he learned that Lazarus had already died and been buried.

Martha heard that Jesus was coming and ran out to meet him. He had not yet arrived at the house, but was still just outside of town. When Martha spoke, her words were full of emotion, yet she was trying to retain confidence in her Master. She said, *"Lord, if you had been here, my brother would still be alive; you would have known what to do to prevent his death. Yet even now I believe that God will give you whatever you ask of him."*

Martha knew that Jesus' power was great and that if Jesus had been present before her brother had died, then he would have seen to it that things would have turned out much differently. But Jesus had not been there. From the way John writes the story it seems that Lazarus must have died shortly after the message was sent to Jesus. And since Jesus was some distance from Bethany, Lazarus was already dead by the time Jesus received the message.

Remember, Jesus had not immediately responded to the message. He told his disciples that he was glad they were not present when Lazarus was ill because through this event God's glory would be seen and from that Jesus' identity would also be known.

After Martha had finished speaking, Jesus told her, "Your brother will rise again."

Martha agreed "Yes," she said, "I know that my brother will rise again in the Resurrection on the Last Day." Yes, she believed in the resurrection. [It seems that in those times, there were two different ways of thinking about death. The Pharisees believed in resurrection; the Sadducees did not. There was something of a disagreement between the Pharisees and the Sadducees on this matter. But Martha agreed with the Pharisees. She believed there would be a resurrection.

Martha's faith was firm. She grieved for the loss of her brother, yet she did believe she would see him on the Last Day.

Isn't that what faith in Jesus is about? Believing that on the Last Day, the Day of the Lord, there will be a resurrection from the dead?

Martha lived her life with the faith that there is a resurrection of the dead that life would continue beyond the grave on the Last Day. The resurrection of the dead would mark the Day of Judgment. Actually Scripture tells us that there are two resurrections —one for the righteous and another for the damned. (John 5:29) Martha believed that.

Yes, Martha agreed with Jesus. Her brother would rise on the Last Day.

We do that, don't we? Same as Martha. We have hope of the resurrection. Our hope of the resurrection is for the Last Day. We know, we believe, in the final triumph of Christ and his final victory. We know we will see loved ones again. We know we will see the Kingdom of Heaven in its fullness, the way that God has planned from the beginning for us.

That's right, isn't it? That's what our hope is all about ... that we'll meet the Lord face to face and live in Glory.

Yes, that is right, but ... there's more, and John's Gospel is telling us Jesus said that Lazarus would rise again. John tells us that when Martha heard that from Jesus, she immediately agreed. She had some consolation in the thought of seeing her brother in the Last Day.

But Jesus went on and said, "I am the Resurrection and the Life. Those who believe in me, though the die, will live, and everyone who lives and believes in me will never die. Do you believe this?

Jesus was not just affirming the idea of the resurrection at the end of time. He was telling Martha that something was about to happen. He, himself, is the Resurrection and the Life. That's different from something that will happen down the road, a long way down the road.

Too often we go through life carrying our slip of paper, telling us about what we consider to be the most important, the things we value most, and among those things we include our faith in Christ, or faith in the Resurrection. We believe, we know, that there will be a Resurrection of the dead on the Last Day. We have that hope for the future.

We mark off the days, though, with the things from the back side of our paper, the things that take our time. Those things mark off the days but don't necessarily have anything to do with the things we value.

The two sides seem so different. We believe that our faith is in the right things, but then we live out each day, having little to do with that side of the paper. We let our lives be filled with the ordinary stuff.

Sounds like a puzzle.

Jesus told Martha, indeed he showed everyone in Bethany that day, that there certainly is more. Jesus showed Martha that he is the Resurrection. We don't have to wait until the last day of the world to see it. Jesus is the Resurrection. He gives life and hope to every day.

Jesus asked where Lazarus had been laid, and he was taken to see a cave where the body lay. There was a large stone over the opening, so Jesus asked that the stone be rolled away. At this point Martha exclaimed that there would be a terrible stench by now, for Lazarus had been dead already four days. By that time the body would have begun to decompose.

But the stone was removed from the grave and Jesus prayed. He thanked God for hearing him. Jesus added that he was praying out loud so that the onlookers would know that he had been sent by God. Then in a loud voice Jesus called to the tomb, *"Lazarus, come out!"*

You can imagine that a hush had fallen on the crowd gathered there, and then there was a great gasp, too, as a noise was heard from inside the grave, the noise of a struggle came from the silence of the tomb. And then there appeared a man bound in the cloths of the grave. His face was still covered with another cloth. It was Lazarus; he had risen from the dead! Jesus had called him from death back to life. He was quickly unbound and given a cloak to cover himself.

Lazarus was alive! Jesus had brought him back to life. Jesus' words were absolutely true. Martha didn't have to wait until the end of time to see her brother again. Jesus is the Resurrection and the Life.

Jesus told Martha, "I am the Resurrection and the Life. Those who believe in me even though they die, will live, and everyone who lives and believes in me will never die.'

When we have faith in Him, Jesus brings hope and health and new life into our world every day.

The message from today's scripture is that Jesus, who is the Resurrection and the Life, needs to be not just on the first side of your page, but on the second side, too. Jesus brings life and new possibilities to our everyday world. We don't have to wait for the final day to see Jesus' resurrection, because it is available to us every day. Do we not say that the moment we come to faith and are justified before God, that is the beginning of eternal living for us? We don't have to wait until we die to begin to live in heaven. We begin living with Jesus from that moment of faith.

Jesus wants desperately to be involved in our ordinary everyday lives: the concerns, the squabbles, the fears, the confusion, the ordinary. When Jesus is in the midst of our everyday life, then the dryness and the boredom of the ordinary are transformed into wonder and blessing every day.

When Jesus was talking to Martha and told her that those who believe would benefit from his life and resurrection, he asked her the simple question, "Do you believe this?"

That's the question for all of us, "Do we believe this? Do we believe that Jesus is the Resurrection and the Life? Do we believe that Jesus gives life to all that we do? Do we believe that Jesus can remake and remold our lives into exciting, wonderful blessings every day?

I have to tell you about a man who discovered this secret in a most unusual way. Or maybe it was more than usual. Brother Lawrence was a monk, but Brother Lawrence had a club foot. He was a clumsy fellow with little natural charm. Although Brother Lawrence aspired to leadership, he found himself in the scullery of the monastery. His job was to scrub the pots and pans and dishes for all the rest of the monks. But Brother Lawrence discovered that, although his job was far from glamorous, and he might never reach beyond his small world, Jesus was with him in the scullery. Brother Lawrence began practicing the presence of the LORD every day. He practiced Jesus' being with him in the ordinary world of kitchen duty. Brother Lawrence came to love his job. It never changed from the same thing over and over again, but to Brother Lawrence it was the most fulfilling job and the best place to be because his LORD was with him right there. His best friend was Jesus. Lawrence knew he was with him right there in the kitchen, and his world was transformed into a blessing. Brother Lawrence never left his kitchen work, but one day a bishop heard about the monk with the really great attitude, and the two began a correspondence through letters. That is how we today can hear about Lawrence's discovery—"practicing the presence of the LORD."

Jesus showed Brother Lawrence that he is the resurrection and the Life. Lawrence discovered that Jesus transforms everyday living into true blessing when he believed and practiced Jesus' presence with him every day.

John 15: 1-8 NRSV

15 "I am the true vine, and my Father is the vinegrower. 2 He removes every branch in me that bears no fruit. Every branch that bears fruit he prunes[a] to make it bear more fruit. 3 You have already been cleansed[b] by the word that I have spoken to you. 4 Abide in me as I abide in you. Just as the branch cannot bear fruit by itself unless it abides in the vine, neither can you unless you abide in me. 5 I am the vine, you are the branches. Those who abide in me and I in them bear much fruit, because apart from me you can do nothing. 6 Whoever does not abide in me is thrown away like a branch and withers; such branches are gathered, thrown into the fire, and burned. 7 If you abide in me, and my words abide in you, ask for whatever you wish, and it will be done for you. 8 My Father is glorified by this, that you bear much fruit and become[c] my disciples.

FRIEND

Life is full of examples of ways people get into bad situations and don't know where to find the answer. They live without hope. That's not living!

In chapter Ten of John's gospel we hear Jesus telling us that he came to give us life and give it to us in abundance. And in today's lesson we hear Jesus saying that he is the True Vine—that we need to abide in him and he will abide in us. Jesus is all about life and living to the fullest. In him we can be all that we were created to be—to be fully alive.

Our scripture today is the final time Jesus speaks of himself as "I am". Previously he has already said,

>I am the bread of life

>I am the living water

>I am the light of the world

>I am the gate of the sheep

>I am the way, the truth and the life,

>I am the Good Shepherd

>I am the resurrection and the life.

Then, finally, in Chapter 15 Jesus says, " I am the True Vine." That is the last of Jesus' I am' statements.

Each "I am" statement shows us a slightly different picture of who Jesus is. Like different facets of a diamond, we learn of different facets of Jesus' identity when he calls himself, "I am."

This final picture of Jesus, the true vine, presents for us a picture of a great plant, having a thick, strong stem from which come branches, leaves, and fruit. The Israelites would have been familiar with that. Grapes grew in nearly all the areas of Judah, and the picture of the grapevine was easy for everyone to imagine.

I think we in Alabama have a similar familiarity with vines, although not necessarily with grape vines. We have kudzu vines, which grow in abundance in our forests. I was fascinated the first couple of years we lived here to see how those amazing vines take over whatever they grow on to. Some of the scenes that are created from the kudzu-covered trees are reminiscent of cookie cutter figures from Disney. Amazing!

The vine is the part of the plant that supports the branches, leaves, and fruit. None of those parts of the plant can live without the support from the vine itself. The vine is the image of life-support for all that grows from the vine.

When Jesus uses the vine metaphor, he is trying to help us understand the nature of our spiritual selves. Our spiritual bodies have needs just as our physical bodies do. Our physical bodies need healthy food and water every day, and so do our spiritual bodies. The vine provides the necessary nutrients for the branches and leaves to live and produce fruit. Without the vine there would be no life for the branches and leaves.

After some talk about how the vine is pruned by the vinedresser, who is Jesus' Heavenly Father, Jesus then says, "Abide in me, and I will abide in you."

The branches on the vine live because they have nourishment from the vine, the source of life. Without the life-giving nourishment, the branches would die. They can't just stop occasionally for a drink at the well; they must stay connected to it.

What is Jesus asking us to do? How in the world can we 'stay connected' to him?

There are two things we do to stay connected to the vine—one which we avoid, the other which we seek out.

The one to avoid might be called 'spiritual garbage", since we're using the metaphor of nourishment for our spirits. Spiritual garbage can be found everywhere in this world. The internet, the T.V., and all media has spiritual garbage in abundance, so it's easy to access if you're looking for it. That does not mean that we must eliminate those wonderful items from our lives, but it does mean that spending time looking at pornography, or watching gambling on T.V., or drinking in visual images of naked people isn't nourishing our spirits.

One of the most sober lines in the Bible, I think, is from St. Paul's comment in the First Chapter of Romans. Paul lists all sorts of evils in this world; then Paul adds, *'they know God's decree that those who practice such things deserve to die—yet they not only do them but even applaud others who practice them.* " 1:32

In other words, we are guilty of the crime if we relish in the thought of it, or if we watch someone else doing it. (That definitely calls into question certain books, magazines, T.V. and videos.)

So first we must avoid 'spiritual garbage.'

The second is to fill ourselves, to drink deeply, of Jesus, the true vine.

We need to be fully connected to Jesus like a healthy branch would be connected to the vine. The healthy branch is not looking for some other form of nourishment, but expects and gets nourishment from the vine.

From where is our spiritual nourishment coming?

Nutritionists tell us 'You are what you eat." That works for our spiritual lives, too. We are spiritually what we feed our spirits.

We stay connected to the vine when we purposefully put ourselves in the places where we can find God. Those places, sometimes are called spiritual watering holes, places where we can drink deeply to feed our thirsty spirits.

Those places are not hard to find. John Wesley used to call them the "Means of Grace".

That would be Bible reading and Bible study Prayer, worship, faithfulness to the sacraments Giving freely and serving others in Jesus' name

As for our thinking, St. Paul sums it up beautifully in his passage in Philippians 4:8 *"Finally, beloved, whatever is true, whatever is honorable, whatever is just, whatever is pure, whatever is pleasing, whatever is commendable, if there is any excellence and if there is any thing worthy of praise think about these things.*

There are many Christians who live with difficulties and challenges and troubles. Christians have hope and joy. They may be experiencing serious physical difficulties, but because they are abiding in Christ, they are living for Jesus. They have joy in their lives because they know that Christ lives in them and is present to them. They have joy right now and they have the hope of Christ in the future. They have faith that God's plan for the kingdom includes living a life without the present physical struggles. They will be healed body and spirit.

These people are living, living in Christ, connected to the true vine.

You may or may not have heard about Joni Erickson Tada. She has every reason to give up, to be angry, to be in despair. Joni managed to break her neck between the 3 and 4th cervical bones when she was about 18 years old. In that instant Joni was changed from a vibrant, athletic young woman who had the whole world of opportunities in front of her to being a quadriplegic. She was totally paralyzed from her neck down. She could move nothing. She could move her neck and her head and her face, but nothing else. Joni did go through a time of despair and wanted to end it all, but one day Christian friends visited her and Joni discovered that she was still connected to the True Vine. She could think and talk and communicate. Joni gradually learned to draw with a pencil and later paint with a paint brush in her teeth. Her art work became world known when she sold it to the UN for Christmas cards one year. Joni learned how to survive in this world, even to pay her own way. Joni today has a 15 minute, daily radio show that is all about helping people who are physically challenged learn to live life more fully by being connected to the True Vine, Jesus the Christ. Joni is a deeply spiritual woman who has shared her faith with thousands, maybe millions, over the years. Her wonderful testimony of goodness and blessings from her LORD has changed the lives of many others. Joni knows that we have to stay connected to the vine; we have to abide in Jesus.

This morning we sang, "I am the church, you are the church, we are the church together. All who follow Jesus, all around the world, yes, we're the church together."

We are the church when we abide in Jesus, when we avoid spiritual garbage and are spiritually nourished by Jesus. We are the church when we gather together to share our faith with one another. To celebrate and be thankful for the great things God in Christ has done for us.

John 15: 26-27 16: 4b-15

26 "When the Advocate comes, whom I will send to you from the Father—the Spirit of truth who goes out from the Father—he will testify about me. 27 And you also must testify, for you have been with me from the beginning.

4I have told you this, so that when their time comes you will remember that I warned you about them. I did not tell you this from the beginning because I was with you, 5 but now I am going to him who sent me. None of you asks me, 'Where are you going?' 6 Rather, you are filled with grief because I have said these things. 7 But very truly I tell you, it is for your good that I am going away. Unless I go away, the Advocate will not come to you; but if I go, I will send him to you. 8 When he comes, he will prove the world to be in the wrong about sin and righteousness and judgment: 9 about sin, because people do not believe in me; 10 about righteousness, because I am going to the Father, where you can see me no longer; 11 and about judgment, because the prince of this world now stands condemned.

12 "I have much more to say to you, more than you can now bear. 13 But when he, the Spirit of truth, comes, he will guide you into all the truth. He will not speak on his own; he will speak only what he hears, and he will tell you what is yet to come. 14 He will glorify me because it is from me that he will receive what he will make known to you. 15 All that belongs to the Father is mine. That is why I said the Spirit will receive from me what he will make known to you.

THE PROMISE

This sermon is going to be hard to hear. At least I believe that nearly everyone here is only partly here. Many of us have our minds on something else, besides praising God, this morning. We've had a really full time recently. There are a whole lot of health concerns, some of them very serious. There's doctors and hospitals and surgery for some. A few of you are really on overload with concerns and worries. We've just been praying about some of the concerns, and they are far from minor. We can trust that God will be present and active in these concerns, but our minds are still there.

Some of us are also thinking about the fact that we Palmers are about to leave. In fact, this morning is our last worship service with y'all. And that thought may be interfering with your mind being on the praise-to-God mode.

What all these various concerns mean is that there's a lot of changing taking place and change always has the added concern of fear or worry. We can't help it. We seem to fear changes and the unknown automatically. We find ourselves, if we're really honest with ourselves, worrying about the future. What will next week or next month bring? How will we manage to get through to the other side? What will it cost? Who is leaving and not coming back? What can I do to make things better? What can I do to survive?

Those are just some of the questions we may be facing. There's a lot of emotion in them.

Would you believe our entire family is moving this summer! Everyone is changing something; four of the five of us are actually, physically, moving from one spot to another. Stephen just moved home from college and then on to his new position at Decatur First UMC. He has his own apartment there in Decatur, as he is working with youth at that church. David, our older son, and his wife, Beth, are about to move to Orange County so David can start his first appointment as a pastor. Leslie and Greg and our grandchildren are moving from Belgium to Montgomery—Maxwell AFB—in July. Dave is about to turn old enough to think about retirement, so he is flirting with various modes of retired behavior. And you know about me. I'm moving to our home in Madison—to live there and commute to my next appointment at Chestnut Grove UMC. So, we're all moving.

That means change. As far as we can tell, the changes we're about to face are pretty positive. Some changes that folks are facing are not fun.

So, when I say that you may be having a difficult time hearing this sermon, I understand.

I have to say I had a hard time getting down to working on this sermon. Maybe I thought, in the back of my head, that if I didn't have a sermon for Sunday, Sunday wouldn't ever come ... But here it is, and I'd better have something for you!

You may know that I usually use the lectionary to guide my thoughts about what I'll work on for Sunday's message. Would you believe that the lesson today, Jesus is saying good-bye to his followers? He was giving them a good-bye address.

Jesus was about to make a great change, and he had to tell his followers about it. Jesus was about to leave them. He was going away. He was actually going to Heaven to live with his Heavenly Father. There wouldn't be any more visiting later on. Jesus was leaving.

He had spent some good time with his followers, and they had learned much. But now it was the time for Jesus to leave. His followers didn't understand; they couldn't understand why he was going. But Jesus knew, and he wanted to help prepare them for his departure.

Jesus recognized his disciples' sadness. Seems the minute he mentioned his leaving they reacted with sadness. No one wanted Jesus to leave. "No", Peter had said, "No! God forbid it!"

But Jesus went on beyond the sadness to say that his leaving was to their advantage. Did you hear that? Jesus said, *'it is to your advantage that I go away, for if I do not go away, the Advocate will not come to you; but if I go, I will send him to you.* (John 16:7)

Jesus gave his disciples a wonderful promise right then, and it is still a wonderful promise for us today.

Jesus promised to send the Advocate, the Holy Spirit of Christ, to come to the disciples and to us.

Do you realize it is because of the Holy Spirit that we even know one another?

It is because I had a profound experience of God's grace that I have followed a path that led to my becoming a pastor. Because I was filled with Christ's Holy Spirit that I have the assurance within me that I must share with everyone I meet.

Let's look back again. Our Scripture in Acts tells us about the day that the Holy Spirit came and filled each of Jesus' followers.

1When the day of Pentecost had come, they were all together in one place. 2And suddenly from heaven there came a sound like the rush of a violent wind, and it filled the entire house where they were sitting. 3Divided tongues, as of fire, appeared among them, and a tongue rested on each of them. 4All of them were filled with the Holy Spirit and began to speak in other languages, as the Spirit gave them ability.

5Now there were devout Jews from every nation under heaven living in Jerusalem. 6And at this sound the crowd gathered and was bewildered, because each one heard them speaking in the native language of each. 7Amazed and astonished, they asked, "Are not all these who are speaking Galileans? 8And how is it that we hear, each of us, in our own native language? 9Parthians, Medes, Elamites, and residents of Mesopotamia, Judea and Cappadocia, Pontus and Asia, 10Phrygia and Pamphylia, Egypt and the parts of Libya belonging to Cyrene, and visitors from Rome, both Jews and proselytes, 11Cretans and Arabs—in our own languages we hear them speaking about God's deeds of power." 12All were amazed and perplexed, saying to one another, "What does this mean?" ¹³But others sneered and said, "They are filled with new wine."

¹⁴But Peter, standing with the eleven, raised his voice and addressed them, "Men of Judea and all who live in Jerusalem, let this be known to you, and listen to what I say. ¹⁵Indeed, these are not drunk, as you suppose, for it is only nine o'clock in the morning. ¹⁶No, this is what was spoken through the prophet Joel:

17 'In the last days it will be, God declares,

that I will pour out my Spirit upon all flesh,

and your sons and your daughters shall prophesy,

and your young men shall see visions,

and your old men shall dream dreams.

18 Even upon my slaves, both men and women,

in those days I will pour out my Spirit;

and they shall prophesy.

19 And I will show portents in the heaven above

and signs on the earth below,

blood, and fire, and smoky mist.

20 The sun shall be turned to darkness

and the moon to blood,

before the coming of the Lord's great and glorious day.

21 Then everyone who calls on the name of the Lord shall be saved.'

So, Jesus promised the Holy Spirit before he left and then, shortly after, the Holy Spirit came.

It is because of the Holy Spirit that you and I even know one another.

The Holy Spirit convened the church. When the church began it was because the Holy Spirit had filled the hearts of Jesus' followers, and called them together. Can you just see them that day, rejoicing, having a laugh in on the streets of Jerusalem? Every one of them chattering away to anyone they could find, telling of Jesus and his wonderful works, especially how Jesus, who had died, was now, once again living.

The Holy Spirit filled each believer with love and joy and peace. They were so excited and thrilled by what the Holy Spirit had done that they couldn't help sharing their joy.

That was the first day, the day the church began. You could call that day the birthday of the church. It began because the Holy Spirit acted in each heart, igniting them, exciting them, and calling them to unite, to come together and love one another.

The Holy Spirit is who calls us together every week, to come and be the people of God here at Gandys Cove, Falkville, AL.

The Holy Spirit is the One who teaches us about Christ and gives us gifts for making church— love, joy, peace ...

Thank goodness for Jesus' promise of the Holy Spirit! It is He who is responsible for us having a church.

I am here with you today, because I had a profound experience of God's grace for me many years ago. That experience has led me to seek leadership in the church, doing many things, and eventually going to seminary and seeking ordination. If I had not discovered the wonderful news of God in Christ, the offer of forgiveness and new life in Christ, I would never have gone to school or become a pastor. Our paths would never have met.

Thank goodness for Jesus' promise of the Holy Spirit. The Spirit is the comforter, who fills our hearts when we are sad or lonely or fearful. The Holy Spirit tells us that we are God's children, and that gets us through the tough times together.

Jesus also tells us that God will be faithful to give us as much of the Holy Spirit as we ask for. The Holy Spirit is the best of all gifts, because it is the gift of Jesus' self, his own spirit within us.

John 17: 20-26 NRSV

20 "I ask not only on behalf of these, but also on behalf of those who will believe in me through their word, 21 that they may all be one. As you, Father, are in me and I am in you, may they also be in us,[a] so that the world may believe that you have sent me. 22 The glory that you have given me I have given them, so that they may be one, as we are one, 23 I in them and you in me, that they may become completely one, so that the world may know that you have sent me and have loved them even as you have loved me. 24 Father, I desire that those also, whom you have given me, may be with me where I am, to see my glory, which you have given me because you loved me before the foundation of the world.

25 "Righteous Father, the world does not know you, but I know you; and these know that you have sent me. 26 I made your name known to them, and I will make it known, so that the love with which you have loved me may be in them, and I in them."

<u>ONE WITH CHRIST</u>

One of the things that is different about Americans from the beginning is our independence. We value our independence greatly. I understand that in times past in other countries, a person was pretty much stuck with doing the same thing the family did. Farmers begat farmers; bakers begat bakers; professionals begat professionals. There was not the freedom of choice for occupations that we have today.

There was no saying, "I'm doing my own thing." The future was pretty much plotted out for children, maybe even before they were born. Their futures were pretty much determined by the families' work and place in society.

But we Americans hear a different drummer today. We truly value being able to choose our own professions and our own way of going about life.

I recently heard a wonderful talk by a Dr. Oz Guinness about our unique position in the world because of what our founding fathers gave us in the First Amendment. They provided 'freedom of conscience' for every citizen, which was an unheard of concept in other countries. Freedom of conscience allowed people to choose their faith, or not to have faith. It allowed freedom of thought, which would have been a big step toward freedom of thought in other areas of life—vocation, marriage, as well as faith. What a remarkable achievement that was!

We view this 'freedom' as a strength that allows us to be able to choose our own path in life. We are exercising our God-given right to choose what we want to do; how hard we will study or work; where we will live; who we will marry; and what G/god we will worship.

Our lesson today, however, is a portion of Jesus' High Priestly Prayer. In it Jesus asks his Heavenly Father that those who follow him will be one with him and the Father, even as He and the Father are one.

Rather than being fiercely independent, Jesus is calling us to be 'one' with Him. Does that present a problem for us? Is that command an infringement on our rights as a free person? Is there some way to resolve this puzzle? How can we maintain our freedom and independence and still respond to Jesus' words and his calling to us?

What is it that Jesus was talking about ... that we be one with him and the Father? How can we be one with them even as he was one with the Father?

I suppose we first need to think how Jesus was one with the Father.

Jesus came to live among us humans for the purpose of doing his Father's will. He told his disciples that he had come to do his Father's will and to complete his work. (John 4: 34)

As Jesus followed his Father's will, God was working through him. Of course the ultimate picture of God working through Jesus was at the cross. We look at the cross as the ultimate moment of revelation of God's love for us and glory for Jesus. Throughout Jesus' life he was doing the will of God; he showed many signs of God's work. Who but God could bring sight to a man blind from birth? Who but God could clean a leper's skin and make it as smooth as a baby's velvet skin? Who but God could bring life to the man's withered limb? Who but God could make the finest wine from well water? Who but God could quell a storm at sea in an instant? Jesus' whole life and ministry pointed to God at work in him. Yet the greatest of all was the cross. It was truly his glory. It showed exactly who Jesus is. It showed us Jesus' closeness to his Father.

Christians can't see Jesus without seeing God's action in him. Those two concepts are inseparable—God acted in Jesus. (There's even a Protestant denomination called the Church of God in Christ—C.O.G.I.C.)

If that is so, then we'd have to say that being 'one with Christ', as Christ is with God, his Father, has to have similar dynamics.

I'd like to suggest several of those dynamics— what it is to be one with Christ:

First we have to carry our own cross. (Matthew 16:24—Jesus says, *"If any want to become my followers, let them deny themselves and take up their cross and follow me."*

First. Our cross is whatever we must do to be Christian. Sometimes it may be difficult to stay the course, to hold firm to our convictions, yet standing firm is the cross we must bear. I don't know that we much think that our life as a Christian as our cross we bear ... and it may not be every moment. But if we are true to our faith, we will find those in this world that are not happy with our Christianity. Our faith may get in the way of someone else's independent thinking. If we are truly trying to do justice, for instance, and there are some who would take away the freedom of others, then we must speak out, even if doing that puts us in a position of discomfort.

We know that there are some places in this world where being a Christian today might lead to prison or death. That is not true here in the Bible Belt today, but because of our lack of danger, we can be greatly tempted to be pretty casual about our faith.

Second, we need to obey Christ. Jesus was absolutely obedient to his Father's will, right to the final moment. He never wavered, even though it cost him everything. Obedience to God in Christ is essential to being Christian.

God calls us to faith before we are all cleaned up and worthy of his love. You could say that we start at "ground level zero". We begin living a life of faith, a life of holiness, from the very beginning. Some of us might start from a very colorful background of blatant fooling around, drinking, gambling, etc. Others of us have not been that obviously sinning, but our sins are still very present. (Maybe we're very busy judging others or gossiping or hanging on to grudges or squandering gifts that God gave us or not using God's gifts to God's glory. There are so many ways to fall short of the Glory of God!

We begin from some starting point and are called to become mature. "Perfect" is the word that Jesus uses in Matthew. (Matt 5:48)

God calls us to be baptized and to learn and obey all his commands. That's a tall order, one that we can't accomplish overnight.

Obedience will be different for each person here. We each have different decisions to make, different neighbors to love, different family members to live and grow with. But our obedience is the same. When we do the will of God, whether it be a life changing decision or a small matter of following God's voice today, we are being obedient.

Finally, Jesus' glory revealed God working and acting in him for the world. Although the Romans and Jews who put Jesus to death had tried to negate what Jesus stood for, God spoke more loudly that Jesus was exactly right.

When we live as believers, as followers of Christ and carry our crosses and live in obedience to God, it is very apparent to the world that we are different. We are definitely marching to the sound of a different drummer. We are following a master that means everything to us. When we live that way, God is revealed in our lives, too.

People can look at our lives and see how God in Christ has made a difference in our lives.

Jesus asked his Father that his followers, those then and those to come, would be one with him, just as he and his Father were one.

That may seem like an impossible concept, because we are so different. How can we be one?

I used to wonder about faith and its being passed on from one generation to the next. If we are on in Christ, what assures that oneness? Is the faith of the first followers of Christ watered down by now?

We certainly see examples of watering down … losing vividness when we replicate things.

When we make copies of things sometimes the multiples come out a little washed out. The ink is limited. The cutting edges are not as clean; the multiples, especially, those that have come after some time, are just not as good as the originals.

However, when we look at the generations, although each new generation mixes the genes a little differently, and the same genes have been around for thousands, maybe millions, of years, each new person has just as strong a body as the first ones. In fact, given improved nutrition and safety, the bodies are even a bit stronger than originally.

Might it be in the same way that the new generations of spiritual people? They are not the watered down clones of earlier faithful, but have the newness and strength of the first disciples. After all, it is not humans alone who are reproducing new faithful people, but the Holy Spirit, the same spirit today as originally, that is giving the faith to the people. No, strong people of faith are as strong today as before.

When we are one in Christ, we are given the same love and Holy Spirit that was given the first disciples. It is in no way inferior to any other. We share the same quality of love as did the first disciples of Jesus. My nephew, Larry was in the hospital this past week. He has found himself to be in a really serious condition, which I pray will have a good outcome. Larry experienced some chest pains last Monday, called his mother, my sister Nancy, and she quickly took him to Cedars of Sinai Hospital. Nancy knew about that hospital and the heart specialists there, because three years ago, just before Larry graduated from high school he got a virus which attacked his heart. He was a very sick young man then, but the doctors said that virus would never return and that there was no permanent damage done.

You have to picture Larry. He's got reddish hair, a zillion freckles, and stands today about 6 feet five. Larry went to UCLA as a volleyball player. We were thrilled with his accomplishments.

My sister called me Monday night to tell us that Larry's condition was deteriorating fast; she was panicky and needed support from family

The best support I can think of is prayer.

I sent out a request for prayers from some of my email addresses. I just zipped down my email list (nice and quick) and pulled out various names that came up and included them on a prayer request list for Larry. These people come from many different faith traditions--Catholic and Protestant-- but each of them is someone I know will pray.

That's when we see our oneness with Christ, when we can join our hearts and minds on behalf of some need. We may be different, even fiercely independent, but we have the freedom to be One in Christ.

That's what Jesus' prayer is all about.

We are one when we carry our own cross and are obedient to Christ. When God can be seen in our lives making Jesus' prayer something that we can use today.

That's exactly what we need here in our church. We need to celebrate our oneness in Christ and agree to pray and work for our community as people joined by the love of God.

John 18: 3-37 NRSV

John 18:3-37 New Revised Standard Version (NRSV)

3 So Judas brought a detachment of soldiers together with police from the chief priests and the Pharisees, and they came there with lanterns and torches and weapons. 4 Then Jesus, knowing all that was to happen to him, came forward and asked them, "Whom are you looking for?" 5 They answered, "Jesus of Nazareth."[a] Jesus replied, "I am he."[b] Judas, who betrayed him, was standing with them. 6 When Jesus[c] said to them, "I am he,"[d] they stepped back and fell to the ground. 7 Again he asked them, "Whom are you looking for?" And they said, "Jesus of Nazareth."[e] 8 Jesus answered, "I told you that I am he.[f] So if you are looking for me, let these men go." 9 This was to fulfill the word that he had spoken, "I did not lose a single one of those whom you gave me." 10 Then Simon Peter, who had a sword, drew it, struck the high priest's slave, and cut off his right ear. The slave's name was Malchus. 11 Jesus said to Peter, "Put your sword back into its sheath. Am I not to drink the cup that the Father has given me?"

12 So the soldiers, their officer, and the Jewish police arrested Jesus and bound him. 13 First they took him to Annas, who was the father-in-

law of Caiaphas, the high priest that year. ¹⁴ Caiaphas was the one who had advised the Jews that it was better to have one person die for the people.

¹⁵ Simon Peter and another disciple followed Jesus. Since that disciple was known to the high priest, he went with Jesus into the courtyard of the high priest, ¹⁶ but Peter was standing outside at the gate. So the other disciple, who was known to the high priest, went out, spoke to the woman who guarded the gate, and brought Peter in. ¹⁷ The woman said to Peter, "You are not also one of this man's disciples, are you?" He said, "I am not." ¹⁸ Now the slaves and the police had made a charcoal fire because it was cold, and they were standing around it and warming themselves. Peter also was standing with them and warming himself.

¹⁹ Then the high priest questioned Jesus about his disciples and about his teaching. ²⁰ Jesus answered, "I have spoken openly to the world; I have always taught in synagogues and in the temple, where all the Jews come together. I have said nothing in secret. ²¹ Why do you ask me? Ask those who heard what I said to them; they know what I said." ²² When he had said this, one of the police standing nearby struck Jesus on the face, saying, "Is that how you

answer the high priest?" 23 Jesus answered, "If I have spoken wrongly, testify to the wrong. But if I have spoken rightly, why do you strike me?" 24 Then Annas sent him bound to Caiaphas the high priest.

25 Now Simon Peter was standing and warming himself. They asked him, "You are not also one of his disciples, are you?" He denied it and said, "I am not." 26 One of the slaves of the high priest, a relative of the man whose ear Peter had cut off, asked, "Did I not see you in the garden with him?" 27 Again Peter denied it, and at that moment the cock crowed.

28 Then they took Jesus from Caiaphas to Pilate's headquarters.[a] It was early in the morning. They themselves did not enter the headquarters,[b] so as to avoid ritual defilement and to be able to eat the Passover. 29 So Pilate went out to them and said, "What accusation do you bring against this man?" 30 They answered, "If this man were not a criminal, we would not have handed him over to you." 31 Pilate said to them, "Take him yourselves and judge him according to your law." The Jews replied, "We are not permitted to put anyone to death." 32 (This was to fulfill what Jesus had said when he indicated the kind of death he was to die.)

33 *Then Pilate entered the headquarters[1] again, summoned Jesus, and asked him, "Are you the King of the Jews?"* 34 *Jesus answered, "Do you ask this on your own, or did others tell you about me?"* 35 *Pilate replied, "I am not a Jew, am I? Your own nation and the chief priests have handed you over to me. What have you done?"* 36 *Jesus answered, "My kingdom is not from this world. If my kingdom were from this world, my followers would be fighting to keep me from being handed over to the Jews. But as it is, my kingdom is not from here."* 37 *Pilate asked him, "So you are a king?" Jesus answered, "You say that I am a king. For this I was born, and for this I came into the world, to testify to the truth. Everyone who belongs to the truth listens to my voice."*

<u>BELONGING TO THE KING</u>

There is a power in this world, a physical power, that is so strong it holds all the bodies in the heavens together. It keeps them from flying apart. The power is called gravity. Yet scientists have dubbed it a "false force".

It is a very strong force, which causes all the bodies in the universe to be attracted to each other, and by this attraction they are held in their systems, allowing planets and other bodies to rotate or follow their orbits.

Gravity is what holds us down to earth, keeping us from flying off into the heavens. Yet gravity does not hold us so tightly to the ground that we cannot move. We actually have much freedom to travel wherever we want.

We've learned how to "defy gravity" in our airplanes. We feel free enough to never even think about how we are held by gravity.

When we suddenly drop something and it falls to the floor, we are once again reminded that gravity always wins.

We know that whatever goes up, must come down.

Gravity is the force that has a grip on this universe that we cannot stop, nor would we want to.

The force of gravity makes the tides work and the air to move, and the rain to come. It is critical to our lives. Its presence shows us the sovereign hand of God at work in our world.

Today is Christ the King Sunday. Our scripture today tells us that Jesus is king. A king born with a purpose. A king whose subjects follow his voice.

We have never had a king in our United States. The idea of having a king is a bit out of our scope of thinking.

Our presidents are elected for four-year terms; a king reigns for life. Some kings have a great deal more authority than a president.

Jesus is not the king of our country, but in our spiritual world Jesus is King. Both Scripture and Church tell us that Jesus is King.

Jesus' kingship is the subject of our lesson this morning. It begins with the scene at the Roman headquarters in Jerusalem.

Pilate, the Roman governor, was beginning to question Jesus about why he had been brought before him. Pilate first asked Jesus if he was the king of the Jews.

Jesus replied that his kingdom was not of this world, but, he continued, *"For this I was born, and for this I came into the world, to testify to the truth. Everyone who belongs to the truth listens to my voice."*

That's sort of a self-description that Jesus made. That he was born to be a king, tells us three things:

1. Who Jesus is,
2. What his mission is and
3. Who his subjects are.

We shall begin with the scene that occasions Jesus' self-description and then look at his three statements.

The first, who Jesus is, tells us that Jesus was born to be king.

The second tells of his purpose as king is to testify to the truth.

Third--those who listen to his testimony belong to truth, belong to him. They are his subjects.

The scene when Jesus came before Pilate was a very tense one. Already, Jesus had been arrested in the garden and tried before the Sanhedrin, at the home of the High Priest.

The Jewish leaders wanted Jesus to die, but they were not permitted to condemn someone to death under their jurisdiction, so they took Jesus to the Roman governor, Pontius Pilate, to get the Romans to sentence Jesus to death.

Pilate had been governor of Judea several years at this point. He had heard about Jesus, this itinerant preacher and healer. He seems to have heard the word "king" associated with Jesus.

The first thing that Pilate says to Jesus is to ask: "Are you the King of the Jews?"

Jesus answered Pilate with a question of his own, "Who told you to ask that, did it come from you or did someone else tell you to ask?"

So Pilate snapped back, *"Do I look like a Jew? Would I be associating with one? Where do you think I got my question? ... This is my own question."*

Jesus answered, *"My kingdom is not from this world. If my kingdom were from this world, my followers would be fighting to keep me from being handed over to the Jews. But as it is, my kingdom is not from here."*

Jesus told Pilate that he indeed has a kingdom, but it is not the sort of kingdom found in this world. Jesus is king, but his kingdom is not here.

Kingdoms have kings, so Pilate asked, "*Then you are a king*?" (Pilate was the Roman representative in the land. He was the governor. It was his job to be interested in political movements there. If there was someone calling himself king, he would be a threat to the Roman authority. He would be a problem to Rome.

Such problems were not tolerated. They were quickly dealt with and removed.

If this man, Jesus, who was a very popular figure among the masses, made a claim on Roman sovereignty, Pilate needed to know.)

Jesus said he was born to be king. Jesus is king, not of some region or land, some country with boundaries. His kingdom is far greater than a country, even greater than all the countries in the world. Jesus' kingdom reaches beyond space and time to the realm that we can't even completely imagine.

St. Paul pointed to Jesus' exaltation when he quoted a familiar hymn of the new Christians when he wrote to the Philippians:

Let the same mind be in you that was in Christ Jesus, who, though he was in the form of God, did not regard equality with God as something to be exploited, but emptied himself, taking the form of a slave, being born in human likeness. And being found in human form he humbled himself and became obedient to the point of death—even death on a cross.

Therefore, God also highly exalted him and gave him the name that is above every name, so that at the name of Jesu every knee should bend, in heaven and on earth and under the earth, and every tongue should confess that Jesus Christ is Lord, to the glory of God the Father.

Jesus said that he came with a purpose. He is the king who went to the far country to reach his subjects. For this purpose, he was born.

He came to announce the truth, to testify to it. That truth was the truth of his kingdom, God's kingdom. Jesus' message was all about the kingdom of God, which he was establishing for the whole world.

His message was about God's love, which is so great that God is willing to go to any extreme to reach to us. Jesus' message was about our being his followers, his disciples, learning to live in the kingdom that we've been invited to enter, the kingdom that will last forever.

Then Jesus said that those who belong to the truth are those who listen to his voice. They would be the subjects in his kingdom.

Those who obey his commands belong to the truth, his kingdom.

Jesus' words in this lesson are almost an exact echo of his words found earlier in John about his sheep.

Remember, Jesus said, *"My sheep hear my voice. I know them, and they follow me."* 10: 27

We might ask ourselves, how do we hear Jesus' voice today?"

How do we know we have heard it ourselves?"

John Wesley would ask, does Christ's spirit witness to your own spirit? "Do you know that you are a child of God?" Are you familiar with the king's voice? Do you know when it has spoken to you?

We need to be aware of hearing his voice. Jesus speaks to us from Scripture, from the pulpit, from fellow Christians, from words you remember from times past.

When you hear Jesus speaking to you, do you take note of his words or do you shut them out, thinking not now. I didn't really hear that, that's not a word for me; That's not the word I want to hear?

For me, as pastor, sometimes the word comes from the church —the North Alabama Conference.

When you go into the pastorate, you have to be willing to hear God's direction for your life coming through the channel of the church, from the bishop's appointments for you.

Last year the word was "wait". That was a bit hard to hear, but the wait did give me a whole year to unpack the furniture and discover our new home in Alabama and get nicely connected to a UMC here.

Last April when Gary, our superintendent, called me to tell me that I had been appointed to Stevenson First we were a bit thoughtful about the distance it was from our home, that it would expect me to live apart from my family.

But this church has become a wonderful blessing for us.

Christ is king. He is king of the greatest kingdom anywhere, anytime, the kingdom of Heaven. Christ is our king, ruling our lives, when we give him that authority.

Jesus has given us the freedom to choose between his kingdom or our own kingdom, our own selfish desires.

Jesus' words to Pilate are a challenge to us today. He told Pilate that those who listen to his voice belong to the truth.

Jesus brought the truth. He brought the kingdom of God to earth for us. We belong to him when we hear his voice and obey it.

Remember the false force called gravity? That force, which holds us to the earth, allows us to move wherever and however we like. Isn't that a great example of Christ's sovereignty?

He allows us to choose how we walk in this life. He has given us much freedom to choose from many possibilities in this world. Yet Christ our King has more force as gravity does.

No matter how far or fast we move along in this world, gravity is still there holding us, keeping us from flying away. Even if we could escape the bounds of this earth's gravity, there is gravitational pull effecting every quadrant of this universe; we can never be too far from it; it always has a pull on us. No matter how far we move from Christ's will, his will remains. It is still there for us; it is still calling us.

I think that God has given us that force of gravity to show us a little picture of how complete God's sovereignty is over this world.

It is absolute and complete; he will be there for us always as sovereign LORD.

Today we celebrate Jesus as King, Christ as King. He is the King of the universe, the sovereign LORD, and we belong to him!

20 *Now on the first day of the week Mary Magdalene *came early to the tomb, while it *was still dark, and *saw the stone already taken away from the tomb.* ² *So she *ran and *came to Simon Peter and to the other disciple whom Jesus loved, and *said to them, "They have taken away the Lord out of the tomb, and we do not know where they have laid Him."* ³ *So Peter and the other disciple went forth, and they were going to the tomb.* ⁴ *The two were running together; and the other disciple ran ahead faster than Peter and came to the tomb first;* ⁵ *and stooping and looking in, he *saw the linen wrappings lying there; but he did not go in.* ⁶ *And so Simon Peter also *came, following him, and entered the tomb; and he *saw the linen wrappings lying there,* ⁷ *and the face-cloth which had been on His head, not lying with the linen wrappings, but rolled up in a place by* *itself.* ⁸ *So the other disciple first come to the tomb then also entered, and he saw and believed.*⁹ *For as yet they did not understand the Scripture, that He must rise again from the dead.* ¹⁰ *So the disciples went away again to their own homes.*

EASTER 101

A man lay in the ICU at Huntsville Hospital. He had been in a terrible accident, a head-on collision—his truck and another car. He had head wounds, including a broken nose, lacerations and contusions, several nasty fractures and his spleen might not make it. The man had been in a coma, but he was coming out of it, finally. It looked as though the man would survive, although he was facing months of recovery ahead of him.

In the morgue in the basement of the hospital lay the body of a young woman. She had been a wife and mother. Her two little girls were in the day care program at my church. Fortunately, although the girls had been in the car at the time of the accident, they escaped injury. Their safety belts held them in, and they survived the crash. Not so for their mother.

The little girls, I think their ages were 4 and 6, were left with only their father to raise them.

I got a call to make the hospital visit to the man. I was asked to make the visit, because the husband of one of our church members was the driver of the truck. He had been driving drunk. He had lost control of his vehicle and crossed the median of the road, colliding head on to the car with the mother and the girls. When the news came to the pastor, he was deeply struck. He was sickened at the unfairness of the accident and the terrible loss that the young family had suffered by the thoughtless snuffing out of the young woman's life.

The pastor of the church could not bring himself to make that hospital call. He found that he was too angry at what the man had done to minster to him.

So I went. As it turned out, I was not allowed into the ICU, where the man lay, because his visitors were being strictly limited and his sister and his wife had both come to visit him, too. I spent time with each of them individually and then time together with them; we talked; we prayed.

As I was beginning to think about this Easter Sunday service and what I might say, for some reason this scene popped into my head. I started thinking about it. The man who lay in the ICU bed, was someone who had really failed; his whole life was a mess. His wife told me some other things about him; the two of them had been having some big problems in their marriage; he'd had an affair; he drank too much. The day of the accident he had ditched work and been with another woman. There wasn't much the man could be proud about.

What did that have to do with our Easter message?

And then I realized ... Jesus died for the man. Jesus died to save him from the sins he had committed. As foul and stupid and really disgusting as we might think of him, he is someone that Jesus loves so much that he died for him.

Could it be that the pastor who couldn't bring himself to visit the man, could it be that he hadn't come to terms with that? Do you suppose he did not realize or believe that Jesus had died for that man and that his sins were forgiven? Maybe he understood it in an academic sense, but at the gut level ... he couldn't

Could it be that the other pastor had not come to terms with his own sinfulness? That might be the root of the thing. Maybe the pastor was a pretty decent person, someone who had really not done much in the way of blatant sinning in his life. It's possible. He's probably not the only one who could be like that. When it comes to appreciating Jesus' forgiveness there is nothing like big, bad, really disgusting sin to clearly show us how obviously needy we really are.

Jesus' offer of forgiveness is better appreciated by those who recognize the gift, because there's no question as to whether it is needed. Their foolish fallenness sticks out in loud, crashing tones that the whole world knows.

Blessed is the one who knows herself to be poor in spirit and welcomes the one who comes in the name of the LORD. That person will be forgiven, because she will ask humbly to be forgiven.

There is serious danger for us if we kind of go along in life without ever recognizing that we are sinners. The danger is that if we don't really believe that we are in need of forgiveness, then we may find that we are still in the camp of depending on our own righteousness, our own self-righteousness. THAT IS A DANGEROUS PLACE TO BE. Because Jesus cannot save us if we don't recognize the need for help. If we drift along merrily not recognizing our need for Jesus' forgiveness, we may find that we cannot forgive others.

The only way any of us can come to minister to another person is as one who knows that Jesus died for us, for you and for me. No matter how disgusting, how painful, how horrid the crime, Jesus still offers forgiveness.

I believe we have to come to realize our own culpability, our own fallenness and neediness, before we can truly minister to others. If we don't, we can find ourselves judging others for their sins, rather than recognizing the great thing that Christ has done for us and them and what he is offering us all.

If Christ can forgive me, he also forgives others, and when the forgiveness is accepted, something wonderful and glorious happens. It is something very much akin to the wonder of the day of Easter, when the women found the tomb empty. The news of the empty tomb sings out in great, thrilling, wondrous tones of the new life offered to sinners just like me. It is good news to me, and it is good news to the world.

The news of being forgiven and getting a new chance in life is like that Easter Day—all things are new again.

- There is freshness in the air
- There is wonder in the soul
- There is a thrill of hope springing up in your heart.

Christ is risen; he is risen, indeed!

We've all heard it said, and maybe we have heard it falling from our own lips, "I just can't forgive So-And-So. He or she did me wrong.' Again and again I run into folks who tell me they cannot forgive; they are holding some grudge. Maybe they are very bitter about something that happened, and they are stuck in the mire or the pain and anger of the offence. Sometimes it almost seems like people rather enjoy holding and remembering grudges. We can easily relate to people feeling that way.

Too often we may be tempted to think that the bitterness that we hang on to is understandable. We are only doing the rational thing, reacting to the way anyone in the same circumstance would. We think, 'What happened to me was not fair. The abuse we experienced shouldn't have happened, therefore we have the right to feel sorry for ourselves or be bitter or angry. Don't we?'

Who could fault us for feeling hurt? Who would say, 'Buck up and get over it?' Who would be so heartless? What unfeeling clod would tell us to not feel the pain that we carry?

But we are called, by virtue of the cross and the open grave, to forgive.

That's a big part of what Easter is all about. It's about forgiveness, about reconciliation and beginning fresh again.

Easter tells us, 'yes, bad things happen; yes, pain is present; abuse and deceit and betrayal and all the rest. Yes, all those things happen in our world, and every one of us will experience them.' Some of us are even the perpetrators, the evil doers, of the wrongs. But Easter tells us that although those evil things happen there is a new day coming; there is a new day TODAY, when God has forgiven each of us and is calling us to take that forgiveness and begin again, afresh. We don't begin afresh as if the pain never happened, but as wiser and more loving people, because we have been forgiven.

Jesus forgiveness is complete. He offered forgiveness for all the wickedness of the world, not just for some.

We make a mistake if we think that what we've done is too bad to be included in the sins that Jesus died for. I know when I was young I used to wonder if the sins that Jesus died for had a limit. Might I sin so often that eventually there would be the one that breaks the camel's back, so to speak, and there would be no more forgiveness?

I may not be the only one who has thought that. But it's faulty thinking.

Just think about who Jesus is. He was mortal, like us, but he is also God. And God is infinite. That is why Jesus, the Incarnate One, was the only one who could die for our sins, because it is his infinite person that forgives. There is no great number that, when reached, finds the end of God's love and forgiveness for us.

Dr. Jay Adams, a Christian counselor, once spoke of a mother and her twelve-year-old daughter who came to see him. The little girl seemed to be troubled; maybe she was acting out at home. As the three of them spoke, Dr. Adams asked the girl if she knew about Jesus and that Jesus could forgive her her sins. The girl seemed to believe that. Then the mother jumped in and told Dr. Adams that she was sure her daughter was a good girl; she hadn't done anything seriously wrong. Dr. Adams turned to the mother and asked her not to downplay the girl's feelings. It was important to take the girl seriously about her sin. If she thinks that God can forgive misdemeanors but can't forgive big, bad sins, then God is not big enough for what she needs.

Are we like that? If we think that God can forgive the little stuff but not the big stuff, we don't understand our God. We limit God's power. God is plenty big enough to forgive all our sins, if we let him.

That may be the deal, right there. We have to let God forgive our sins for them to be forgiven. Christ offers us the forgiveness, through unmerited grace, but if we don't accept it, what good will it do us?

Jesus once told a Pharisee that those who are forgiven much would also love much. He was referring to the woman who came in off the street and ministered to Jesus by weeping over his feet and drying her tears with her hair. When we realize who much Jesus has forgiven us, we are freed to love others more than we ever could in our natural selves.

The message of the empty tomb is we are forgiven. The message is not meant to be complicated, that only some, who are clever, can understand. It simply says, God loves us and has forgiven us, so that even though we have sinned, there is a way out. There is a way to start over again and do better this time.

One morning on the first day of the week, very early, before the sun began to rise, the women were awakened by the sounds of the waking world. The birds were singing that morning. The day before had been cold and dark and stormy. It matched their moods, for they had been gripped with deep mourning for their LORD. But this new day dawned with beauty. The day itself spoke of a new day and new hope, but they may not have considered that; remember, they were in great pain.

As they came to the garden where the tomb was, suddenly there was a great earthquake and an angel came from Heaven and rolled away the rock from the opening of the tomb. The guards were so fearful they shook and fell over like dead men, but the angel told the women not to fear. He said, "I know you are looking for Jesus who was crucified. He is not here; he has been raised. Come, see where he lay."

The tomb was empty! The body had been there, but it was gone! That's one of those moments that takes time to sink in. The evidence of Christ's rising was right before them, yet it must have taken time for them to recognize what they had just witnessed.

Jesus was alive!

- The message of the empty tomb is very simple
- It sings out a wondrous fact to the world
- No grave could keep Jesus
- Jesus is alive
- He had risen from the dead!

The message of Easter is about new life

- God gave life to Jesus
- God raised him up to live eternally.

The message of Easter is that God forgives us.

- Because of Jesus' suffering and death, God forgives us.

The message of Easter is that Jesus saves us.

- He is the one who has given us new life
- New hope and a new reason to live

Easter is the day that recognizes Jesus for who he is—

- The Son of God
- The one who has all the power and authority over the world.
- Easter is the Divine proof of God's love.

CHIRST IS RISEN   HE IS RISEN, INDEED!

FAMILY PICTURES

I'd like us to begin this morning by thinking about friends. Friends are such a gift. Some are new and some we have had for a long time, but friends are valuable. And friends are people that we hold in our heart. We treasure them there. And we know that if something happens to our friends we are immediately concerned. If we lose our friend, maybe to death, we are hurt, perhaps deeply hurt. We know when friends have become important to us, because when they are gone, we hurt deeply.

When families get together, especially at special times like reunions, we try to get lots of pictures. Family pictures tell us about the state of the family when the picture was taken. We can see the ages of the kids and who made it to the event. Family pictures give us a frozen moment in history of the family. Lots of memories are stored in the pictures.

Our last family picture was taken at our son David's wedding last July in Casper, WY. My folks were in the picture as well as Dave's sister Jackie and her husband, Frank. Of course the bride and groom were at the center of the picture, but there were Leslie and Greg, seated at the feet of everyone else, each holding one of our grandchildren for the picture.

Our scripture this morning is the Easter story in John; we know it well. But you might not know that in that story Jesus tells Mary Magdalene that she has been included in the most important family—the family of God. Jesus said, "I am going to my Father and your Father, to my God and your God." The family he's talking about is the heavenly family of God. Jesus, the Son of God, the second member of the trinity, has just included Mary and the other followers, including us, in this family.

Family pictures tell us that we belong to a family. We have a place in the family, a place at the family table. We know that membership in our family gives us purpose and identity.

We know all about families. Life would be very different without our family. Families are a wonderful source for us for nurturing for encouragement, for help and guidance, not to mention great fellowship, and opportunities for celebrating life. Our families are terribly important to us. They are a wonderful gift from God.

The family that Jesus told Mary about early that Easter morning was about an even more important family—his family, in which he has included us. It is our real family, because it is the family that we will be living with for a long time—even eternity.

This morning I want us to look at some family pictures, God's family pictures. The pictures I have in mind are about how we got included into the God's family. I will use four pictures. Each one will show us a little different aspect of the family.

The four include:

> The First Picture
>
> The Bookends Picture
>
> The New Picture
>
> The Family Picture

The first picture was Mary's picture. Mary was the first one at the tomb that morning. She had made her way to the tomb as early as she could; her purpose was to dress the body of her lord for burial. There had been no time for those niceties on that Friday afternoon. Everything had to be done in haste as the Sabbath was approaching. When Mary saw the stone rolled away from the entrance of the tomb, she supposed that the body inside had been stolen, and she raced back to tell the others.

Peter and John took off running as soon as they heard her news. Then Mary followed them, making her way back to the tomb again.

The second time she saw the open tomb she looked inside and saw two angels dressed in white sitting on the ledge where the body had been. They exchanged a few words, and then Mary turned back. As she turned she saw a man, whom she took to be the gardener and she questioned him about the body.

Did he know anything about it?

Did he know where it had been taken?

Where could she find it?

The man then called her name, "Mary". And she knew, she knew then, it was Jesus' voice calling her name. Mary knew that he was alive again. She knew that somehow he was standing there before her, talking to her.

Mary cried out Rabboni—teacher! And started toward him. But Jesus cautioned her, saying, "Do not hold on to me, because I have not yet ascended to the Father. But go to my brothers and say to them, 'I am ascending to my Father and your Father, to my God and your God.'"

The first picture was full of emotion, running, surprise, and thrill. There was no understanding, just pure joy at seeing Jesus alive.

Jesus gave Mary important words to pass on to the others—they were all now part of the family of God; just as Jesus was a member of the family, so, too, were the followers and those who heard about this marvelous new arrangement. It was a picture that Mary would repeat to everyone who would listen to her for the rest of her life.

The second picture is the 'bookends' picture. By that I mean that the events of that morning were the perfect complement of the events that had happened on Friday before.

The two events were the Crucifixion and the Resurrection. The two events cling to one another like members of a perfect set. It is impossible to consider one without the other. The two, the Crucifixion and the Resurrection, are the bookend events that caused this new family arrangement. We don't really have exact words to explain how it is that we have been incorporated into God's family, but we know that it was during that time that it all happened.

The deal was sealed. The plan was executed. The promise was fulfilled.

Jesus told us that the many prophesies in the Hebrew Bible were about him; the prophesies told that the Messiah must suffer for the good of many. His crucifixion was part of a great plan to bring humans into His family. The Resurrection was the moment that revealed that truth. The Crucifixion, when Jesus followed his Father's will perfectly and allowed himself to suffer so terribly, provided the means for our being invited into his family. The Resurrection told us it was so.

That brings us to the third picture—the new picture.

What Mary found that morning was something completely new. Mary found an empty tomb. The dead body of Jesus was not there where she expected it to be. Then on her second trip to the garden, Mary met the LORD and they spoke. Jesus was alive; he was not dead.

Such a miraculous event could not be explained by normal understanding. Such an event had to be an act of God.

St. Paul tells us that God can create something out of nothing and can call the dead back to life. That is something that God only can do. There is no power on earth that can do what God did in Jesus.

Surely we have seen examples of people being resuscitated after some terrible event stops their heart and breathing. Resuscitation is well known in our time today, but everyone who has been resuscitated, brought back to life from a sudden death, dies later of some other cause. If a person has been resuscitated they are just as mortal as everyone else.

But Jesus was given resurrected life--that is life that cannot die. It is immortal life. Only God can do that.

The Resurrection of Jesus has been likened to the greatest event in history—creation. We can't compare Jesus' resurrection to anything else, but this new act of God. The third picture is God doing something completely new.

The final picture is the family picture.

When Mary met Jesus in the garden, she didn't even realize she was seeing him immediately. But then he called her name and everything changed. When Jesus called Mary's name she suddenly knew he was no longer dead but alive. She also had no reason for the enormous grief that she was feeling. Suddenly everything had changed. Joy began to overcome the grief she had been enveloped in.

Jesus told Mary that she and the other followers had changed even more than she realized because they were now all part of his own family. He told her to go tell the others.

The fourth picture is the family picture. Jesus was telling Mary that we have been made members of the greatest family there is.

This news that Jesus gave Mary that Easter morning was very good news. Being a member of the family, being included in the family picture, gives us life that is eternal. It gives us access to the Holy Spirit and to God's power. Being a member of the family gives us a new identity and purpose.

We are part of that family when we see God in Jesus; when we hear the story of what God did in Jesus and believe it. St. John tells us that when we believe that God acted in Jesus for us, we are given the privilege of being called the children of God. There It is—family members. (John 1:12 *But to all who received him, who believed in his name, he gave power to become children of God.*)

I want end this sermon with an illustration that comes from Alan Weatherly, pastor of Asbury. He told a story about a young man, a college student who was a champion diver.

The young man, I'll call him Phil, was not a man of faith. In fact he pooh-poohed others that were believers. He thought the whole idea of God was a big joke and told his friends just that. He wanted nothing to do with the "family of God."

Phil was pretty full of himself. He was an excellent diver; his studies were good; he knew he was on his way to big things. Life was treating him well.

Phil had some Christian friends who shared their faith with him, but Phil was hard. He wouldn't believe. He shrugged off their encouragements to consider faith in Jesus.

He had attended a Christian rally at his school with these friends, but he didn't respond to the message or the invitation to give his life to Christ. Phil had heard the good news, but he resisted. He just didn't think it was for him; he didn't think he needed religion in his life.

Phil found himself pretty wound up inside the day after the rally. It was evening, and he decided to go over to the swimming pool and take a few dives to relax himself.

The pool was located in the big swimming hall. It was dark by then. The full moon shown through the windows into the Olympic-sized pool. Phil put on his swim trunks and walked up to the high dive ladder. He ascended to the top of the ladder and walked onto the board. This was very familiar to Phil. He had walked out on this same board many, many times. Although it was pretty dark in the room, the glow of the moon showed through the window and lit up the wall behind the high dive board. Phil walked to the end of the board and turned around backwards to begin his stance for making his first dive. As he stood facing the wall with his arms outstretched he saw his shadow on the wall.

His form stunned him that moment, because instead of seeing his own shadow he was seeing the form of the crucified Christ on the wall, or so it seemed to him. Phil suddenly realized what his friends had been saying, that Jesus died for him on the cross. He realized that the words he'd heard at the rally were for him, too. He realized that Jesus loved him and was beckoning to him to come. Right then and there Phil made a decision to follow Christ, and he knelt on that unlikely spot, on the high dive board and gave his life to Jesus.

That moment Phil was filled with the wonderful sense of God's presence and his love and peace. Phil was a new man and he was full of joy. He thought he would make that dive now as long as he was already up on the board. So he stood up and assumed the pose in order to take the bounce and make a backwards jack knife into the pool below.

Just at that moment, though, the janitor walked into the big hall and snapped on the lights. The room was flooded with light and Phil looked down at the pool, which was illuminated now. As he gazed into the pool he saw something that made him clutch. The pool had been drained! There was no water in it. What Phil had almost dived into from the high dive was an empty pool. If he had jumped a few minutes previous, before the lights had been turned on, Phil would have made a tragic dive into an empty pool.

Phil's prayer, giving his life to Jesus, made him a member of the family of God just a moment before, had literally saved his life a moment later. Phil realized that God was already acting in his life to give him life, life in abundance. What a picture for the family of God, as a new member joined the family.

FAITH FINALLY FOUND

How often have we heard the saying, "better late than never?"

That could apply to all sorts of things.

My sister, Stevie, didn't have her first child until she was 38 years old. Today she's the mother of two, very active, beautiful children. <u>Better late than never</u>.

Irmi Roessler and I sang together in the Methodist Church choir in downtown Wiesbaden. Irmi had been a maiden lady for most of her life, until she had married the widowed husband of a good friend of hers who had died. Irmi was in her fifties when she and Eckhart married; they have been happily married 20 + years now. Better late than never.

There are plenty of folks that go back to school for some degree in order to pursue a new career field. They may begin late, but they really enjoy the work they have dreamed of doing for so long. Better late than never.

And so it goes with faith. Some people don't come to faith in Christ too very early in their lives; they are like the workers in the vineyard who didn't sign on to work until the last hour of the day—but … They'll get paid just the same as the full-day workers. <u>Better late than never!</u>

Thomas was late, too. Scripture tells us that Thomas wasn't with the rest of the believers when Jesus made his first appearance to them. So when Thomas arrived where the others were, and they told him about Jesus' coming to them, he didn't believe. Thomas told everyone that he would not believe that Jesus was really alive until he could put his own finger in the nail holes in Jesus' hands and place his own hand in Jesus' wounded side. It he could do that, then he might believe.

Thomas was full of doubts.

We all have doubts. We doubt many things. We doubt ourselves, our abilities. We doubt we can afford something or that we should try some new idea. Some of us spend a good deal of time doubting.

We doubt our world, when it's unfriendly; we even doubt God, sometimes. Deep inside we may worry that doubt is wrong. We may think a Christian should never doubt. A Christian should be strong in the faith. A Christian should be a great example of faith for others. What should we do if we discover that doubt has stepped into our lives?

I call this sermon FAITH FINALLY FOUND. I believe that doubt is good for us, and doubt can make us stronger believers, but we have to work through the doubt to find God's gift of faith.

Since we all think differently, we have different ways of working through our doubts.

This morning we shall begin with Thomas, who has so often been labeled "The Doubter," and we shall see that though he doubted, he was open to evidence that might lead him to greater understanding and finally to faith.

Then we shall turn to two men who were serious doubters in their early lives; we shall see how they, too, placed themselves in the way of hearing or discovering the truth of God's love.

Lastly, we'll turn to us and consider three spiritual watering holes that can lead us to finding our faith.

Thomas missed out on the excitement. He was off by himself, hurting terribly, after all that had happened that day. He had been so sure of himself, so sure of his master-- his friend, Jesus. And he had been so bold earlier. Thomas had recognized that if Jesus returned to Judea his life might be in danger, but Thomas announced to all the followers that he would go to Jerusalem with Jesus and die with him if necessary. Such boldness!

But when it came to the night of Jesus' betrayal and capture, Thomas and the others held back and only watched on as Jesus was taken away and finally crucified

Thomas couldn't believe how badly he had acted. He had been so afraid; he just ran away. Now he hurt so badly, on so many levels, he didn't know what to do. He hurt because he missed his lord. He hurt because he had not done anything to help him. He hurt because he had run away. He hurt because Jesus had suffered so terribly. He just hurt in every way.

Finally, the pain had almost numbed, and Thomas found his way back to where the others were. He expected they were pretty much in the same boat as he was. Hurting just the same.

But Thomas was greeted in a strange way. Everyone was happy. That didn't make any sense. Everyone was even joyful. They were certainly not in the deep funk like he was. His first thought was that they were all a bit drunk or had gone a bit nuts in their grief.

Then he heard. They all told him at once. They said that Jesus had met them in that room; he was alive! Thomas heard their words, but they didn't make sense to him. He knew that Jesus had died; he was really dead. He couldn't believe what they were saying. No, he didn't believe.

So Thomas told them all, "Not until I put my finger in the hole in his hands; not until I place my hand in his wounded side will ever believe what you say."

Then, suddenly, Jesus was with them, again. He spoke, *"Peace be with you."* Then he moved to where Thomas stood and invited him to touch him to touch and see for himself that Jesus was alive.

Thomas stood riveted to his spot, not moving for a moment. Then it all came together for him, as he began to realize the truth of what his friends had just told him. Jesus really was alive.

Thomas then spoke the words that have echoed through the ages since. He looked at Jesus and called him, *"My Lord and My God"*.

Thomas moved from doubt to faith in one dramatic moment. We don't really know how long all these things took. Seems like the scriptures are always shortening events and conversations. It could have been several, very pregnant minutes that lapsed as Thomas was putting this altogether. Then his announcement spoke words that have come to be the words we use for Jesus—our Lord and our God. Thomas was bold to speak his faith in Jesus, once it all came together for him.

Thomas has often been described as "The Doubter," the one disciple that hung back from instant belief, but Thomas had essentially the same response as did the other followers the first time they met Jesus, the risen Lord. When the women returned from the tomb and announced Jesus' rising, they, too, doubted.

Doubt today is a bit different, though. What the followers doubted was amended when they met Jesus face to face. That isn't happening in the same way today.

Do you know that some really great Christian writers we've known were atheists or agnostics during their early years? I've always wondered what it was that brought them to faith.

Both these men had a Christian parent and were exposed as children to Christian faith. But each of them, for different reasons, wandered away from the faith; it was some time before they found it again.

C. S. Lewis--Author of The Screwtape Letters, Mere Christianity, The Chronicles of Narnia—The Lion, The Witch, and the Wardrobe. Was an atheist for many years as a young man. He was a scholar of the English language, a professor at both Oxford and Cambridge Universities. For Lewis the world revolved around words and knowledge and rational thinking. His doubt swirled around many philosophical arguments, which he enjoyed having with fellow scholars. But as time wore on, Lewis made some discoveries.

He began realizing that there were some absolutes, or recognized truths, in the world that he believed in. The idea of fairness, of freedom, of truth. Where did these ideas come from?

Then Lewis began to realize that the people for whom he had the greatest respect were Christians; he began to see that the non-Christian writers he read were really intellectual light-weights, lacking real depth in their works.

Very gradually Lewis came to realize that there was a God. On that day, he felt as if he was taking off a very heavy suit of armor and was now free to believe.

Lewis once wrote: "If you are an atheist you have to believe that the main point in all the religions of the whole world is simply one huge mistake. [On the other hand] Christians are free to think that all religions have at least some hint of the truth."

With the dawning of belief in God, Lewis worshiped weekly at a church nearby. He thought he should be honest about his new belief and worship this God, now that he was willing to ac-knowledge Him. Lewis' faith in Christ came about a year after he first believed in God.

It seems that through this long quest, Lewis had finally seen the nail prints and wounded side of his Lord. He finally found the faith to know that Jesus was his Lord and his God.

 Fulton Oursler, editor, author of The Greatest Story Ever Told, had been raised Protestant by his parents but fell away from faith. He spent much of his early life delving into various world religions and even science. It was on a trip to the Holy Lands that Fulton thought he might write a book called A Skeptic in the Holy Land. He published that book, and that was that, or so he thought. But the subject would not go away. Following the Second WW, Fulton began thinking that the ethical statements of Christianity should be brought before for the world to see. So he conceived a book, which would be "an elevator boy's life of Jesus, making it really interesting, like a magazine serial." Thus, he began work on The Greatest Story Ever Told. What began as a several-week project to pull together the basic story lo Jesus' life became a great adventure; Fulton returned to the Holy Land and walked in the same places that Jesus had walked. The names and places he visited suddenly became very real for Fulton. This journey to the Holy Land marked the moment of truth for Fulton. His faith was ignited; it was finally found, and he realized that this was not just some old tale. The Greatest Story Ever had become his story.

I asked myself, what is it that has caused me to believe? That has caused me to follow the Lord Jesus? To take him as my Lord?

There are three things that have instilled faith in me. They are like three great watering holes for my spirit. When we are thirsty, we want water, nothing else will quench a thirst for water. We can read about water; we can learn all about water from many sources, but unless we can go to the river or the well and draw out water for ourselves, our thirst won't be quenched.

The three are the faith of others, the Bible, and God's faithfulness to me.

The faith of other Christians is the first watering hole.

Sometimes I learn of others from reading their stories and marvel at how God has worked in their lives, changed their lives so wonderfully. Like the writer of Hebrews says, there is "so great a cloud of witnesses" that speak loudly of their own faith and lead us to faith ourselves.

And then there are the lives of many good friends I know, who know Jesus as their Lord. Some of them have had quite dramatic changes in their lives because of finally finding faith in Jesus.

Your faith, too, is important to me. As I learn of your faith, learning how God has worked in your life, it strengthens mine.

The Bible is a key watering hole. After all, it is rich in faith stories. It is our sourcebook where we can learn the dramatic stories of people, even long ago, who walked in faith with God. Spending time in the Bible is a wonderful source for filling up the void left by the world. Along with that, for me, is sitting at the piano and playing/singing through the good old songs in our hymnal. Such spiritual refreshment.

The greatest river/source of all is God's Holy Spirit, who quenches our thirst when we ask him. The third way my faith has been affirmed is by the Holy Spirit's work in me. When I begin to think of all the Holy Spirit has done for and in me, I am awed. God, the Holy Spirit, has healed me so many times, I've almost lost count. God has also healed my wounded spirit and forgiven me for so much. Through this life I've known God's healing and forgiving and care.

These three-- Christian friends, the Bible, and the Holy Spirit have been my spiritual watering holes and my opportunity to see the signs of Jesus' resurrected body, to know that Jesus is alive and in my life.

Yet some of us do doubt. Honest doubt is a good thing. We've seen how it can lead a person to a strong faith and commitment to the LORD. Lewis and Oursler took different journeys before they finally found faith.

Lewis might tell us to relax, stop working so hard at all the rational stuff and throw off the heavy coat of armor of doubt you may carry; be free to believe and enjoy it.

Oursler could tell us to return to the Holy places in our lives, relive the stories of faith and the music and the pictures. Drink in those wonderful images and give thanks to God for your faith.

 Finally, Thomas would tell us that when we see Jesus for who he is, we will see God moving and being in him, and we, too, will know that Jesus is our Lord and our God. Amen.

John 21: 1-19

21 *Afterward Jesus appeared again to his disciples, by the Sea of Galilee.[1] It happened this way: [2] Simon Peter, Thomas (also known as Didymus[1]), Nathanael from Cana in Galilee, the sons of Zebedee, and two other disciples were together. [3] "I'm going out to fish," Simon Peter told them, and they said, "We'll go with you." So they went out and got into the boat, but that night they caught nothing.*

[4] Early in the morning, Jesus stood on the shore, but the disciples did not realize that it was Jesus.

[5] He called out to them, "Friends, haven't you any fish?"

"No," they answered.

[6] He said, "Throw your net on the right side of the boat and you will find some." When they did, they were unable to haul the net in because of the large number of fish.

[7] Then the disciple whom Jesus loved said to Peter, "It is the Lord!" As soon as Simon Peter heard him say, "It is the Lord," he wrapped his outer garment around him (for he had taken it off) and jumped into the water. [8] The other disciples followed in the boat, towing the net full of fish, for they were not far from shore,

about a hundred yards.[c] 9 When they landed, they saw a fire of burning coals there with fish on it, and some bread.

10 Jesus said to them, "Bring some of the fish you have just caught." 11 So Simon Peter climbed back into the boat and dragged the net ashore. It was full of large fish, 153, but even with so many the net was not torn. 12 Jesus said to them, "Come and have breakfast." None of the disciples dared ask him, "Who are you?" They knew it was the Lord. 13 Jesus came, took the bread and gave it to them, and did the same with the fish. 14 This was now the third time Jesus appeared to his disciples after he was raised from the dead.

15 When they had finished eating, Jesus said to Simon Peter, "Simon son of John, do you love me more than these?"

"Yes, Lord," he said, "you know that I love you."

Jesus said, "Feed my lambs."

16 Again Jesus said, "Simon son of John, do you love me?"

He answered, "Yes, Lord, you know that I love you."

Jesus said, "Take care of my sheep."

17 The third time he said to him, "Simon son of John, do you love me?"

Peter was hurt because Jesus asked him the third time, "Do you love me?" He said, "Lord, you know all things; you know that I love you."

Jesus said, "Feed my sheep. 18 Very truly I tell you, when you were younger you dressed yourself and went where you wanted; but when you are old you will stretch out your hands, and someone else will dress you and lead you where you do not want to go." 19 Jesus said this to indicate the kind of death by which Peter would glorify God. Then he said to him, "Follow me!"

THE MESSAGE

A man lay in the ICU at Huntsville Hospital. He had been in a terrible accident, a head-on collision, his truck and another car. He had head wounds, including a broken nose, lacerations and contusions, several nasty fractures, and his spleen might not make it. The man would survive, but he was facing months of recovery ahead of him.

In the morgue in basement of the hospital lay the body of a young woman, a wife and mother. Her two little daughters, who had been in the car at the time of the accident, had escaped injury. Their safety belts held them in, and they survived the crash. The little girls, I think they were four and six years old, were left with only their father to raise them.

I got a call to make a hospital visit to the man. It seems that the reason I was called to make the visit was that the driver of the truck was the husband of one of our church members. He had been driving drunk. He had lost control of his truck and crossed the median of the road, colliding head-on into the car with the mother and her two little girls. When the news came to the senior pastor of my church, he was deeply struck. He was sickened by the thoughtless snuffing out of the young mother's life. The senior pastor of the church could not bring himself to make the hospital call. He realized he was too angry at what the man had done.

I made the hospital call. As it turned out, I was not allowed to go into the ICU where the man lay, because his visitors were being strictly limited. His sister and his wife had both come to see him. I spent time with each of the women, individually and together. We talked; we prayed.

As I was beginning to think about what I might say to you today, I knew it must be an Easter message [this being Easter season], for some reason this scene popped into my head. I started thinking about it. The man, who lay in the ICU bed, was someone who had really failed. His whole life was a mess. His wife had shared some other things about him when we talked. She and her husband were having big problems in their marriage. He'd had an affair; he drank too much. The day of the accident he had been with another woman. There wasn't much the man could be proud of.

What does this story have to do with the Easter message?

And then it dawned on me...Jesus died for that man, too. Jesus died to save him from his sins. As foul and stupid and disgusting as we might think of the man, he is someone that Jesus loved so much that he died for him.

Could it be that the pastor, who couldn't bring himself to visit the man, could it be that he hadn't come to terms with that? Do you suppose he did not realize, or believe that Jesus had died for that man, and that his sins were forgiven? Maybe he understood it in an academic sense, but maybe not at the gut level.

Could it be that the senior pastor had not come to terms with his own sinfulness? That might be the root of the thing. Maybe the pastor was pretty decent person, someone who had not done any really blatant sinning in his life. He might not have realized that Jesus sacrificed himself for all sinners, both great and small. Jesus' blood covers all our sins. No Matter What!

A couple of years ago I noticed a church in Huntsville called IMPACT had put out some very large billboards around town. They read, 'God isn't mad at you … no matter what! [God is not mad at you … no matter what!] I also noticed those same words had been printed in very large print across the top of every other page in the whole Yellow Book. That amounts to a lot of pages … and a lot of money invested in that ad.

I got curious about the church, so I did some research online to learn about it. It has quite a ministry, complete with schools, counseling services, youth programs, etc. It's international.

The founder of the church says he's offering everything that a traditional church offers except 'that tired condemnation junk!"

When we hear, 'God is not mad at you ... no matter what,' it's a distortion of the gospel message.

- We Christians know that God loves us NO MATTER WHAT!
- That doesn't mean that we do nothing wrong
- Or that God doesn't care what we do
- Or that God doesn't have a better plan for us.

God loves us and offers to forgive us our failings, and God is calling us into fellowship with Himself. He is also calling us to grow in love for Him and for one another.

We are called to change, to be better today than we were last week, and better still in tomorrow.

We Christians are people who have been reconciled to God through the blood that Christ shed on the cross. We are reconciled people who live together in a community of reconciliation. We see that we have been forgiven a great debt and realize that we are now free to forgive others anything they have done against us.

When it comes to thinking about Easter, the first thing we need to do is to understand the context, the scene, that was surrounding that day.

The situation was dire. It was worse than miserable; it was probably one of the worst, most depressing times for a whole group of people ever in history.

Jesus' followers were gathered in the Upper Room. Each was suffering from the same problem. They had lost. They had lost greatly. They had hoped that their friend, their Master, their beloved Rabbi, was something more than he turned out to be. He had given them such good reasons to believe in Him. Never had such a man been on this earth before. Never had there been one so wise, so caring, so challenging, so wonderful, so powerful, so able to speak great thoughts before. He was so ... good!

They loved him so. He was a good man. He was a great man. He was attractive on so many levels. He was young and strong and so much more. They had hoped he would be the leader they needed so badly to run the Romans out of their country—to rid themselves of their Roman oppressors.

He was perfect in every way, yet now he was gone.

He hadn't just disappeared; he was killed by a terrible, tortuous death ... death by crucifixion. It was bloody and gory ... and unthinkable. It was tragic that he had suffered such a death ... somehow it all just happened.

Then there was the guilt. Each one of them felt it one way or another. When the time came and the danger appeared, they had all fled for their lives. They had run wildly into the night, trying to save their own skins. So there was guilt enough to go around for everyone. Some even hurt more than that because Jesus had predicted that they would fail him. [Such was the case for Peter.]

They were not unaware of grief, the kind that comes when someone close to you dies. But Jesus' death was even harder for them. The grief was mixed with all those other emotions, and they found they could barely do anything but weep and dissolve into a puddle of tears. How could Jesus have died? How could that have happened? When death happens you want to reach out and knock someone's block off. There was anger pent up inside, too. When death happens anger is a new companion.

It's very important to understand this scene, how Jesus' followers were feeling, to get the picture of the first Easter. They were all together, but they were hurting deeply. They had lost their hope.

Easter dawned for Jesus' followers. We've heard many, many times the wonder ot that day. Jesus showed himself to be alive to the women and then to Peter and John and those in the Upper Room, and to the two travelers on their way to Emmaus. Jesus was alive! He had a lengthy dialog with the travels on the road; he spoke and ate with those in the Upper Room. He was clearly alive, and suddenly those who had been in such pain had no more reason for their pain!

Oh, to be a fly on the wall, as they say. Wouldn't that have been a great moment to be there? To say they were shocked is a great understatement. They couldn't believe their eyes. There stood the One whom they loved, whom they were grieving, the One who had disappointed them so.

It was like Jesus healing Lazarus ... multiplied many times over. They were all being called back to life from the death they had been in. They were struggling with their own grave clothes, as the reality of the miracle of Easter began to dawn on them and sink in. Their whole reason to despair and mourn had been taken away.

It was a new day for each of them, a new and glorious day! They were alive, and it was good. They were filled with the joy and love and wonderment of Jesus' love. Their despair vanished as they found new life within themselves.

The first miracle of Easter was Jesus rising from the grave. There was a second miracle, too. It was the miracle that happened that evening in the Upper Room, when life was given back to Jesus' followers. When they saw Jesus showing them that he was alive, everything changed. They were transformed by joy in that moment.

They certainly didn't understand all that had just happened. It would take thinking and meditating about it for years to being to understand what had happened, but two things they knew: Jesus was alive, and they were alive, again, too!

Isn't that one of the greatest proofs of the resurrection—the change that took place in the people? They moved in an instant from suffering greatly to being filled with joy. That's not possible unless it all happened as Scripture tells us it did. Those people changed in that moment to spend the rest of their lives telling others about it. It was that important; it was that remarkable.

I'd like to share a story I heard from a professor from Perkins Seminary in Dallas. The story was about the professor when he was a child.

He said he remembered that when he was young his mother collected S&H Green Stamps. [Do you remember them?] Each Friday evening it was the boy's job to fetch the stamps that had been stashed in the pocket of the car and to bring them into the house and stick them in the stamp books. After some time, several months, the boy and his mother would take the books to the Green Stamp Redemption Center to trade them for merchandise.

On one such trip to the center the boy saw a great, stuffed tiger sitting high on the shelf. He immediately fell in love with the tiger and wanted to take it home with him. But the cost of the tiger was more stamp books than he and his mother had. The boy's mother promised that they would save up more stamp books and come back and get the tiger.

Time passed, and finally the day came when the boy was able to get the tiger. It was wonderful day, as the child finally held the tiger in his arms. The tiger was finally his!

At this point the professor pointed out that the tiger had no way of knowing how much the child loved him, but the tiger now belonged to the boy.

The tiger hadn't done anything to merit the child's favor, but that didn't keep the child from loving the tiger and wanting to have it. And when the tiger was finally his, the boy did not say to the tiger, 'I have done everything necessary to free you from your bondage, go now and do whatever you like. No! The boy loved the tiger and had bought him and the tiger now belonged to the boy.

Jesus bought us for a price. We belong to him. He is not saying to us, 'Go along now and do whatever you'd like. Just remember that I love you.' Too many folks think that's all there is to it. You go out one day and 'get religion'. You say a prayer, and you're saved. There's more to it than that!

I began this sermon by reading about the risen Jesus meeting Peter and several of the other disciples on the beach. Jesus took a walk with Peter down the shore and asked him … three times, 'Do you love me?'

And we know that Peter answered his Lord each time, 'Yes, Lord, I love you.'

Jesus then commanded Peter, 'Feed my lambs … take care of my sheep … feed my sheep.'

Isn't that the deal? Jesus went to a lot of trouble to set things up for us. He bought us for a price, a very dear price. We belong to Him, but he is not just patting us on the head and saying, 'Well, you're free now. Go and do your thing.'

No! Jesus is telling us, just as he commanded Peter, 'Feed my sheep, tend my lambs.' In whatever manner the opportunity presents itself, that is our business, our response to our LORD: to be feeding and tending and caring for those he puts in our path!

Amen.

www.ingramcontent.com/pod-product-compliance
Lightning Source LLC
Chambersburg PA
CBHW071212090426
42736CB00014B/2793